Blooming Patchwork

A CELEBRATION OF APPLIQUÉ IN QUILTS

By Deanne Eisenman

Blooming Patchwork
A CELEBRATION OF APPLIQUÉ IN QUILTS

By Deanne Eisenman

Book Editor: Donna di Natale
Book Designers: Tom Dolphens and Jo Ann Groves
Photography: Aaron T. Leimkuehler
Illustrations: Lon Eric Craven
Technical Editor: Christina DeArmond
Photo Editor: Jo Ann Groves

Published by:
Kansas City Star Books
1729 Grand Blvd.
Kansas City, Missouri, USA 64108

First edition, first printing
ISBN: 978-1-61169-144-3

Library of Congress Control Number:
2014949404
Printed in the United States of America by
Walsworth Publishing Co., Marceline, MO

To order copies, call StarInfo at (816) 234-4473.

KANSAS CITY STA[R]
QUILT[S]
Continuing the Traditi[on]

DEDICATION

Dedicated to my husband, Craig and my children, Ali and Mitch.
Their love and support feeds my creativity.

ACKNOWLEDGMENTS

Many thanks to all those who helped make this book a reality. Especially to my machine quilters: Annette Ashbach, Mindy Prohaski and Jean Miller and to my pattern testers: Kari Lippert, Crystal Marie, Nancy Noah, Elen Morell and Grace Blanchard. Also, much gratitude to my editor, Donna di Natale for her patience and wonderful guidance. Finally, thanks to my circle of quilting friends: especially Vickie, Barb, Annette, Teresa, Jacque and Linda for their opinions and advice over the years.

Thank you to The Hatchery House Bed & Breakfast, Wes[t]
Missouri, for allowing us to photograph the projects in [this]
lovely bed and breakfast[.]
www.hatcherybb.[com]

ABLE OF CONTENTS

ABOUT THE AUTHOR

Deanne took a beginner's quilting class over 20 years ago and has loved the art of quiltmaking ever since. She began designing her own patterns when she could not find what she was looking for in a quilt shop. This led her to begin her quilt pattern design company, Snuggles Quilts, in 2003. Deanne has been successfully self-publishing quilt patterns since beginning the business and continues to market them to quilt shops and distributors to be enjoyed by quilters everywhere. Several of her patterns have been published in major quilt magazines and calendars. Deanne has previously authored two quilt pattern books. This is her first book with Kansas City Star Quilts.

Deanne works from her home studio in Osage, Iowa. Her husband, Craig, has been a great support to her business and even helps when Deanne sells her designs at the International Quilt Market. Deanne and Craig have two children, Ali and Mitch, who had to put up with mom yelling "not with those scissors!" a time or two while growing up. Snuggles the cat is the company namesake since she seems to take ownership of all the quilts that come out of the studio. She often "stars" in blog posts on Deanne's website and is quite a hit. Designing quilts, writing patterns and books, and running the pattern company has been the best job ever. For Deanne, it's great to go to work every day and do something she loves!

Deanne's blog and pattern line can be found on her website: www.snugglesquilts.com.

INTRODUCTION

My Love of Scrap Quilting Meets Appliqué

My style of design has always been influenced by the appliqué from antique quilts and from traditional blocks. Most of my inspiration comes from books documenting quilts from past centuries. I am more drawn to those quilts than plain pieced quilts. I have always loved the look of "orderly chaos" found in sampler quilts, especially if there is an added border of appliquéd vines, leaves and flowers. Early quilters who used worn out clothes or bits of fabric left over from other projects may have thought they were only creating a utilitarian item, but the explosion of color within each block breathes life into even the simplest design. Add some unique appliqué motifs to those pieced traditional or utilitarian quilts and you have my style!

Today, these early quilts are easily re-created with the assortment of fabrics available to us. I have to admit, I have a preferred type of fabric. I cannot pass by a shelf of Civil War reproduction fabrics without stopping! One of my favorite things is to build a stash of many different colors and prints. You don't have to buy one or two yards of fabric to start a stash. Fat quarters, and even fat eighths, are a great way to get variety into your collection. In fact, these pre-cuts, along with strips, are what I use most often to create the scrappy blocks and the appliqué motifs found in my quilts.

When I learned to quilt, over 20 years ago, I did everything by hand, even the piecing. Shortly after those early classes I moved on to machine piecing and quilting but I was still drawn to working with a needle by hand. That is why I decided to take a needleturn appliqué class. Once I began adding appliqué to my projects, I found that it gave a unique identity and added my personality to otherwise common or traditional quilt blocks. As an added bonus, it is a great way to use up fabric scraps. Over the years, this habit of combining traditional blocks with eye-catching appliqué motifs has grown into my style.

I like to think of my appliqué quilts as my own works of art that may someday influence another quilter. I would love to make you an appliqué "convert" if you do not already enjoy the technique. Too often I hear quilters say they are afraid of the "A" word. There is no need to be. I also love appliqué for its portability. I take sewing along on road trips all the time.

This book has several unique, colorful projects to get you stitching your own work of art. Some were inspired by appliqué styles of the past, but all reflect my personal appliqué style. Choose a project, get started and enjoy!

What is Appliqué ?

The word appliqué is from the French word *appliquér*, meaning "to apply" or "to put on." That makes sense since appliqué is the process of layering and stitching pieces of fabric on top of a background fabric or pieced block to create a unique design.

Although appliquéd items date back as early as the 9th century, my focus is on appliqué in America and how it has changed through the centuries. American appliqué quilts have evolved from early broderie perse medallion style quilts to complicated album quilts (think Baltimore Album quilts) to what they are today. I will take you on a tour from the 18th century through the present, showcasing different styles of appliqué quilts and what influenced the women who created them. However, my tour only scratches the surface when it comes to the rich history of this craft. To delve deeper into any one of these topics, check out the many great quilt history books, including those listed in my bibliography. Many of the quilts from previous centuries that survive today are truly works of art and serve to inspire us. The influence of appliqué styles from past centuries is evident today, whether the quilter is reproducing an antique quilt or making their own creation.

Early Appliqué in America – 18th Century to early 19th Century

Few colonial women in the 18th century had time to express their artistic talent by making quilts. Most quilts were made for everyday use. It was not practical to make a quilt that could not be used for anything but decoration

Center Square for Quilt or Bedcover by John Hewson Block-printed cotton plain weave, Early 19th century 32 x 32 inch. Philadelphia Museum of Art: Gift of J. Arthur Ewing, 1967

because fabric was scarce and very expensive. Decorative quilt making was reserved for women of wealth who had more leisure time than the typical colonial settler. Early quilts were mostly whole cloth quilts because, according to many historians, quilters wished to preserve the whole piece of fabric. Large pieces of costly fabric were cherished.

Appliqué quilts that survive from this time period were not used as everyday quilts. Because of the expense, a woman who wanted to make a decorative appliqué quilt used a technique

called broderie perse, a techniq[ue] primarily practiced by women i[n] England, using chintz fabric wit[h] printed designs. They would cu[t] out designs from the expensive fabric and stitch them to a larg[e] inexpensive piece of backgroun[d] fabric. Early chintz fabric from India was printed with Indian-influenced designs. Later, India[n] fabric companies began using items found in English art, such [as] baskets, urns, trees, flowers an[d] birds. A popular early design w[as] the Tree of Life.

Broderie perse was brought to America by settlers in the

coln Album Quilt, Maker: Vera Crosier Bartak; Circa 1968.
lection of the Illinois State Museum. Gift of Vera Crosier Bartak.

l 18th century and quickly
ame popular. It enjoyed great
ularity in the south in the
ly 19th century because many
orted chintz fabrics came
ough the port of Charleston.
se quilts became even more
ular in America when domestic
tile mills began producing
ir own chintz fabrics. In the
ly 19th century, there were
ntz fabrics manufactured solely
broderie perse quilts. John
wson, a Philadelphia printer,
ame known for creating printed
els for mid century quilt tops.
e of his famous panels featured
ower filled urn surrounded by
ds and butterflies.

lost broderie perse quilts
re medallion style quilts, the
minant style of quilt in the early
h century. These quilts had a

central appliquéd motif framed
by a border or borders designed
to complement the appliqué. The
central motif might be a whole
printed panel or pieces cut from
panels and repositioned into a
new design. The borders were
also cut from a printed chintz
fabric or constructed from a small
pieced pattern such as a sawtooth.
Another style of border contained
more appliqué, including vines,
flowers and leaves.

Broderie perse is still used today
to make beautiful quilts. There
are many new fabrics printed with
large-scale flowers, birds or other
designs that quiltmakers cut out
and stitch to a plain background.
The look of an antique broderie
perse quilt can be created this
way, although the effect now
is generally done using fusible

webbing and machine stitching
instead of hand appliqué.

Medallion quilts also remain
popular today, whether the central
motif is pieced or appliquéd.
Borders are then added to frame
the center. The borders can be a
mix of plain, pieced and appliqué.
One example of a modern
medallion quilt is the Round
Robin quilt. Most Round Robin
quilts have a central design with
multiple borders, both pieced and
appliquéd. Round Robin quilts
are quite popular today as a small
group activity. One quilter makes
the center of the quilt and then
passes it on to the next to add a
border. This continues until all the
quilters in the group have had the
chance to add to the quilt.

A Change in Style – Block Style Quilting

Toward the mid 19th century,
the country was expanding
westward, causing great economic
and social changes. A change that
affected quilting was the increased
fabric production by American
mills. This lowered the cost of
domestic fabrics and made them
widely available. Quilting was no
longer only reserved for women
of wealth. Needlework became a
traditional female skill to showcase
a woman's creativity. The wider
variety of fabrics allowed women
to create more unique and colorful
appliqué blocks, something that
was not possible with the limited
designs found on chintz fabrics.
Many more quilts were produced
during this time than in earlier
years.

Quilts were present in everyday
life in the mid-1800s. They
provided comfort and warmth to
children and adults. Utilitarian
quilts were used as linings for
westward bound wagons to
keep out the wind and rain.
Also, breakable items were often
wrapped in quilts for the journey.

7

Once a family arrived on their new homestead, their quilts would often serve as doors and windows for the family's cabin.

Quilting styles began to shift away from medallion style quilts to block style quilts. Of the many types of block style quilts, friendship quilts and album quilts were the most popular, with album quilts being the most likely to contain appliqué. These quilts were often made to tell stories or for special occasions such as weddings, births and fundraisers. Pennsylvania German settlers helped to influence the move away from medallion style quilts by creating appliqué blocks based on traditional German motifs. As they moved west and shared their designs, these motifs began to dominate many of the appliqué quilts made during the 19th century.

Friendship quilts were often used to raise money or made as keepsakes for families moving from a community, usually to travel to a new home in the west. Generally, friendship quilts were made up of identical blocks signed by various people who were important to the recipient of the quilt. The blocks were made by one person or by several individuals. Signatures were either embroidered or signed in ink. The friendship quilts that survive today were probably not used like the utilitarian quilts of the 1800s, especially if they are in good condition.

Some album quilts were signed like friendship quilts but usually included a variety of blocks, each often made by a different person. Album quilts could also contain both pieced and appliquéd blocks. The most famous album style quilts are Baltimore Album quilts. These brightly colored quilts became popular in the mid 1840s but were on their way out by the early 1850s. It was common for

Baltimore Album Quilt
Maker Unknown; Circa 1850 - 1860, 96" x 96" International Quilt Study Center & Museum.
University of Nebraska, Lincoln, 1997.007.0300

these quilts to have twenty–five appliquéd blocks, each featuring unique and intricate designs. Baltimore was a wealthy seaport and one of the country's largest cities in the mid 19th century. Many quilts reflected the growing industry of the city with blocks that featured ships, trains and large city buildings, although they still contained traditional appliqué blocks with baskets, wreaths and floral motifs.

These quilts were works of art and rarely used. In fact, they were often only taken out of storage for special occasions and then carefully stored again. Some historians believe that two women from Baltimore, Achsah Goodwin Wilkins and Mary Evans, made great contributions to

this genre of quilting. Historian Dena Katzenberg theorized that Mrs. Wilkins designed and commissioned many of the Baltimore Album quilts. She also thinks that Mary Evans may have been an apprentice of Mrs. Wilki and also designed and sold bloc for these quilts. Since so much work went into each block in a Baltimore Album quilt, it is very likely that a single quilt was the work of many talented women, as noted by quilt historian Elly Sienkiewicz. She has considered that the name "Mary Evans" was used to represent the work of a group, not a single individual. S believes that if one woman were make a Baltimore Album quilt, w all of its intricate needlework, it would have taken her a full year

rking on it forty hours a week.
s seems unlikely since their
ght of popularity only lasted
ut six years.

altimore album quilts still
aze quilters today. There are
ny who like to reproduce these
lts on their own or by using
ck-of-the-month kits created
today's designers. There is
n a Baltimore Appliqué Society,
nded over 30 years ago to
serve these quilts and promote
art of appliqué.

Moving Toward Industrial America – Mid to Late 19th Century

any advances in technology
ected quilting during this
e period. Innovation in
rics, sewing machines and
nsportation contributed to the
tinued growth in popularity of
lting. This time period is also
dited as the birth of many of
block patterns and quilt styles
popular today.

he first synthetic dye was
urple aniline dye, called
uveine, invented in 1856 by
liam Henry Perkin, an English
emist. As more synthetic dyes
ame available, textile mills
ld produce a wider variety of
rics. Because these dyes were
s expensive, synthetic dyes also
de fabrics more affordable.

lthough there were many
empts to invent a machine
t would sew, most of the early
wing machines in Europe and
erica failed. The first American
tent was issued to Elias Howe in
46, but it was Isaac Singer who
ented the first mass-produced
mmercial sewing machine in the
50s. Because of a patent fight
tween Howe and Singer over
o invented the lockstitch used
the machine, both men shared
the profits from the growing
ustry. Though early home

machines were sold in the 1860s,
the most reliable machines arrived
in the 1870s and 1880s. The first
practical electric sewing machine
was sold by the Singer Sewing
Machine Company.

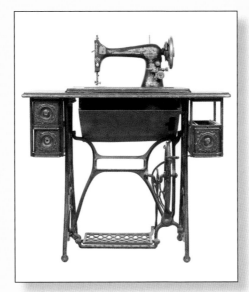

Early Singer Sewing Machine

The railroad expansion westward
made fabrics available to just
about everyone in the country.
Fabrics could be shipped from
textile mills to stores across the
continent faster and for much less
money than before. The savings
reduced the cost of fabric for the
quilt maker as well. More and
more, purchased fabrics, instead
of scrap fabrics, were used in
making quilts.

One style of appliqué quilt that
became popular in the mid 19th
century was the red and green
quilt. These were prevalent around
the time of Baltimore album quilts,
but enjoyed a longer a life span.
Like other appliqué quilts of the
time, these were influenced by
Pennsylvania German settlers. A
white background was common
for the appliquéd red and green
motifs. According to historians,
the background of these quilts was

Red and Green Appliqué Quilt
Maker unknown. From the collection of Terry Clothier Thompson

9

white because large amounts of fabric were needed to make them and un-dyed cotton was the least expensive fabric available.

Today, true red and green quilts from this era appear as if they also included yellow or blue fabrics, but that is because until fabrics were produced using more stable synthetic dyes, the green fabric often faded to these hues and reds sometimes faded to brown or pink. Some quilters did add other colors such as yellows and oranges. These quilts were made up of either one repeated appliqué block or as a sampler with many different blocks. Red and green quilts that had four large appliqué blocks were also popular at the time. The Whig Rose and Rose of Sharon designs are two of the more popular appliqué motifs from the mid-1800s. Many red and green quilts were made using this pattern. The Pennsylvania Dutch-influenced motifs of hearts and tulips are also found in many red and green quilts.

Crazy Quilt circa 1890, Maker unknown. From the collection of Donna di Natale

In the last part of the 19th century, the Arts and Crafts movement, which began in England, took place. This movement emphasized decorative arts and design and was thought to be a reaction to the industrialization taking place in America. Fears and uncertainty of how everyday life would be affected by industrialization inspired designers to look to the past and revive handcrafts from earlier times. Reflecting this movement, early crazy quilts, made with simple fabrics like cottons, flannels and wools, began to emerge in the 1870s and were seen as a departure from the ornate Victorian style of the time. It is also thought that crazy quilts were influenced by a fascination with the Japanese culture. The 1876 Centennial Exposition, the country's first official World's Fair, featured a very popular Japanese pavilion. Historians believe that "crazies," as they were sometimes called, were inspired by the crackled appearance of the glaze found on Japanese ceramics.

These quilts were a move away from orderly blocks

to a more random expression of creativity. However random these quilts looked, they were usually well planned and were a reflection of the quilt maker's personality and talent for design. Some crazy quilts were influenced by the orderly block quilts from earlier in the century. These had "crazy" blocks that were squared and stitched together to make the quilt instead of an overall random pattern. Others had an appliqué medallion center framed by a pieced "crazy" border, or a border of "crazy" blocks. As their popularity grew, crazy quilts became another example of "best" quilts made only for show and rarely used. They were displayed over the backs of sofas or on tables and considered conversation pieces. Most of these quilts were not layered and quilted like today's quilts. If they did have a backing, the quilt was usually tied.

Women used fabrics such as silk, velvet and taffeta for these fancy crazy quilts, instead of the more common fabrics used for earlier quilts. Some quilts had appliquéd ribbons, sequins and intricate beadwork and featured fan motifs that reflected the Japanese influence. Crazy quilts showcased the quilt maker's skill with beautiful embroidery stitching that framed the random pieces of fabric. In most cases, the embroidery was not the original design of the quilt maker but was found in a book by outline embroidery designer, Kate Greenaway. Designs from the book were traced onto the quilt top and used as a guide for stitching the embroidery.

The crazy quilt fad was sustained by an increase in the supply of silk and a decrease in its cost, partially due to increased trade with China in the 1880s. Some shop owners began to package discarded scraps of silk from manufacturers into scrap bags to sell to customers. There were even crazy quilt kits and mail order patterns. With a decrease in popularity by the end of the century, crazy quilts became less decorative. They were once again made with less expensive fabrics and were more often used daily instead of just for display.

Unique Cultural Styles Emerge

Along with the well-known styles [of] quilts from the 19th century [dis]cussed earlier, there were [oth]er styles that emerged from [dif]ferent cultures and regions in [Am]erica. Three distinctive styles [tha]t included appliqué in the [de]sign were Hawaiian quilts, Native [Am]erican quilts and African-[Am]erican quilts.

Hawaiian Quilts

[T]he time frame of when the [uni]que Hawaiian style appeared is [no]t clear, but it is thought to be [bef]ore the 1870s. In the early 19th [ce]ntury, missionaries who traveled [to] the islands introduced quilting [to] the native population. They [tho]ught if they taught the Hawaiian [wo]men this skill, typical to ladies [on] the mainland, it would improve [the]ir behavior in all aspects of their [life]. They began by teaching the [wo]men piecework, but the women [we]re not inspired. Quilt historian [Stel]la Jones believed it was [be]cause the Hawaiians thought it [wa]s a waste of time to cut larger [pie]ces of fabric into small pieces [an]d then sew the pieces back [tog]ether, to once again end up [wit]h a larger piece. They preferred [the] appliqué technique that was [als]o taught. These appliqué skills [hel]ped to foster the creation of the [dis]tinctive Hawaiian style later in [th]e century.

[T]here were two types of quilt [sty]les unique to Hawaii. The first [wa]s called a flag quilt. These were [ch]erished family keepsakes that [we]re only shared with important [fri]ends and guests. The quilt was [m]ade up of a central appliquéd [m]otif framed by pieced Hawaiian [fla]gs. It was thought that these [qu]ilts were an expression of [lon]ging for the kingdom that [ce]ased to exist once the islands [be]came a United States territory.

The second appliqué style is one that is immediately recognizable to quilters today as the two-color silhouette quilt. When you look at Hawaiian quilts, think of the grade school pastime of folding and cutting paper to make snowflakes. This is the basic concept behind the Hawaiian design that is still practiced today. The quilter begins with a large piece of fabric folded in eighths onto which they trace a design. The design is cut out and then appliquéd to a plain background, usually white, creating a large central motif. Some Hawaiian quilts also include smaller appliqué pieces or borders that are cut out using the same technique as the center design.

Historically, most Hawaiians paired either red or blue with a white background for stunning two-color quilts. Some quilters reversed the colors, using a dark color background with a white appliqué motif. A likely inspiration for designs found in Hawaiian quilts were native plants found on the islands. These quilts were heavily quilted, often echoing the central motif across the background. Like the flag quilts, these "best" quilts were rarely used and were carefully stored by a quilter's family. This was partially due to the moderate Hawaiian climate that eliminated the need to use quilts for warmth, and also because Hawaiians believed the quilt maker's spirit became part of the completed quilt.

Hawaiian Silhouette Appliqué Quilt, Maker Unknown; Circa 1930-1950, 85 x 81.International Quilt Study Center & Museum University of Nebraska, Lincoln, 1997.007.0111

Native American Lone Star Quilt with Floral Appliqué,
Maker, Margaret Ogahmahgegedo, Circa 1912, 66 x 75. Frances L. Hanes, gifted in 1985. Courtesy of
Michigan State University Museum, 6814.1 Photo by Doug Elbinger

Native American Quilts

As with the Hawaiians, Native Americans were also influenced by European settlers when it came to quilting. Native American women were thought to have picked up the skill by watching the wives of soldiers make quilts in the many forts as the country expanded west. Missionaries whose ultimate goal was to convert natives to Christianity also taught them the skill of quilting, along with other traditional homemaking skills. Even though they created many traditional quilts with the patterns and styles taught by the white Americans, Native American women soon developed their own style.

One of the most famous quilt patterns that they fused with their own style was the Lone Star design, also known as the Star of Bethlehem. It was similar to a star motif, representing the Morning Star that had been used for centuries to decorate their clothing and other items. They believed the path of this star, which traveled across the sky throughout the year, connected those living here on the earth to their ancestors and to their descendants yet to come. These quilts often had floral appliqué motifs between the star points. The Native Americans were also known to make pictorial quilts that expressed their spiritual and cultural beliefs and values. These quilts were made up of appliqué motifs that sometimes told a story stitched to a plain background and expertly quilted.

For Native Americans, these quilts were often highly symbolic and became a cherished family heirloom. They were used to decorate walls and given as gifts. They were also used in a more utilitarian way to cover windows and doors, on beds for warmth or to comfort the sick.

uch less is known about African-
erican quilts for many reasons.
lts made by these women while
y were slaves often remained
n the owner's family, making it
d to identify who actually made
m. The few quilts they kept with
m in their slave quarters did not
vive the day-to-day use or were
troyed. Also, their white owners
ly recorded the names and
sessions of slaves. Many claims
: a quilt was made by a slave,
oost its importance, have been
ven untrue.

uilting was not a skill these
nen brought with them from
ca, although they were very
led weavers and sewers. This is
most of the quilts that survive
ay show more of a European or
erican influence; they learned
t making after they arrived here.
y in the 19th century, slaves
were freed and returned to
ca often took the art of quilting
k home with them. Since they
e influenced by their American
ners, many slaves made quilts
reflected the popular styles of
19th century. Therefore, it's
unreasonable to believe that
ny of their appliqué quilts were
lallion quilts, album quilts and,
r in the century, crazy quilts.

ome of the few African-American
liqué quilts that survive today
called story or pictorial quilts,
ilar to some Native American
lts. Each appliquéd block in these
lts tells a complete story, often
ed on the Bible. Two of the most
ious story quilts were made
larriet Powers, a former slave
netimes referred to as the mother
African-American quilting. Harriet
born into slavery in 1837 in
ens, Georgia. She likely learned
juilt and appliqué from her
ther. Once freed from slavery,
riet remained in Georgia with her
ily and worked as a seamstress.

er first quilt to be displayed at an

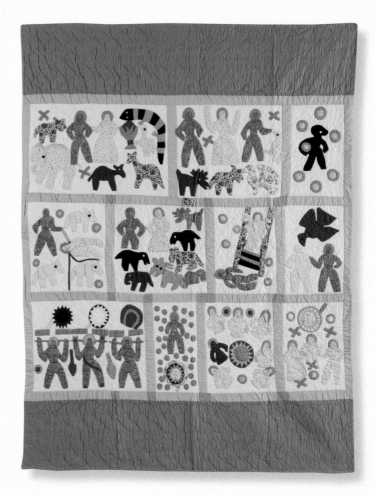

Reproduction Bible Quilt, Made by American Pacific Enterprises in concert with the Smithsonian Institution, 1992. From the collection of Donna di Natale.

Athens fair in 1886 was "discovered" by a teacher and artist named Jennie Smith. Jennie wanted to buy the quilt, but Harriet refused to sell it for several years, until she later needed the money. When she delivered the quilt to the new owner, many quilt historians believe she relayed the stories for each block to Jennie, who faithfully recorded them. This quilt can now be found at the Smithsonian's National Museum of American History. Shown here is a Smithsonian-licensed reproduction of the Bible Quilt, made by American Pacific Enterprises in 1992.

Because Harriet gained some fame for her Bible quilt, she was commissioned to make a quilt in 1898. This quilt, similar to her first, is called the Pictorial quilt and can be found in the Boston Museum of Fine Arts.

Harriet Powers

20th Century Revivals

Talk of "revivals" seems to imply that quilting disappeared altogether as an art form or favorite pastime. This may be true for some parts of the country at certain periods during the 20th century. Women in cities, who enjoyed greater access to modern day advances and store-bought goods, quilted less. However, in rural areas, slow to receive these advances, it appears that quilting enjoyed a more steady popularity. Many credit these rural quilters for keeping the art alive. Some quilt historians believe there was more than one revival in the first half of the century, while others believe the ups and downs of the craft's popularity were all part of only one revival.

As the popularity of the Arts and Crafts Movement of the 19th century continued into the new century, quilters moved away from the excesses of the Victorian era. Show quilts, like crazy quilts, were seen as out of style dust collectors and carriers of disease, although autograph album quilts remained popular as fundraisers. People romanticized colonial America and the simple furnishings and quilts from that time. Women who inherited their ancestor's patchwork or appliqué quilts proudly displayed them and soon copied them using 20th century fabrics. In the early 1910s, patterns began to appear in magazines more frequently and museums began to display antique quilts as art. Some quilters regarded these events as the beginning of the first quilt revival. During World War I, women were encouraged to make quilts for home use, instead of buying manufactured blankets that were needed for the American soldiers overseas, and this also helped to renew the interest in quiltmaking.

Another revival in quiltmaking that appeared to take place in the 1930s was influenced by several events. During the Depression, many people lost their jobs, leaving little money for household items and leisure activities. Quilting with scraps served

Sunbonnet Sue quilt top, Maker unknown.
From the collection of Terry Clothier Thompson

to entertain women and allowed them to provide their families with bed covers, since they could no longer purchase them. The Works Progress Administration (WPA), created to employ people during the Depression, also had programs that taught and promoted arts and crafts, including quiltmaking. In 1933, the city of Chicago celebrated its 100th birthday with the Century of Progress exhibition. As part of this fair, Sears, Roebuck & Company held a national quilt contest that thousands of women entered, helping to increase the popularity of quilting. Even though some women quilted to pass the time during World War II, the craft appeared to decrease in popularity again. With

the men away at war, women went to work to provide for the family a keep the post-Depression econom growing. After the war was over, many women stayed in their jobs and had less time to quilt.

Interest in quilting began to grov again in the 1960s, which quilt historians believe was the start of revival that continues today. Like t earlier Arts and Crafts Movement, this revival was fueled by quilters looking to simpler times to escape problems of the modern-day worl Sentimental quilters revived the traditional quilt patterns of the pa using newer fabrics. Other quilters were inspired to create works of art not meant to be used but to be

layed, almost reminiscent of the
w quilts of the 19th century. The
t continued to grow through the
0s, helped along by the country's
ntennial celebration. Through
last decade, new techniques,
erns and some new styles, such
rt quilts, have kept the art of
ting alive, ushering it into the
t century.

pliqué in the 20th Century and Beyond

rly in the 20th century,
liqué quilting gained popularity
the help of a quilt designer
n Indiana named Marie
ster. Because she disliked
y of the popular designs of her
, she began to design her own
t patterns. Her flower gardens
ed as the main inspiration
these designs, helping her
reate realistic floral appliqué
ts. Webster was known for
g pastel colors, made available
advances in the fabric dyeing
ustry, instead of the darker
rs of the past century. As
most quilts in the early part
he 20th century, her appliqué
ts were both block style and
lallion style quilts.

the early 1900s, when
jazines started to solicit
inal pattern designs from
ters, one designed by Mrs.
oster was the first to be
lished in The Ladies Home
rnal in 1911. She also wrote
of the first known quilt pattern
ks in 1915, titled "Quilts, Their
y and How to Make Them."
s book remains available today.
designs required a great deal
kill to reproduce, helping to
ate a demand for her patterns.
s demand led her to begin her
pattern business in 1921,
Practical Patchwork Company,
ch sold her patterns and fabric
. Other pattern companies
ved floral appliqué patterns
n the 19th century and began
ing kits as well. As appliqué

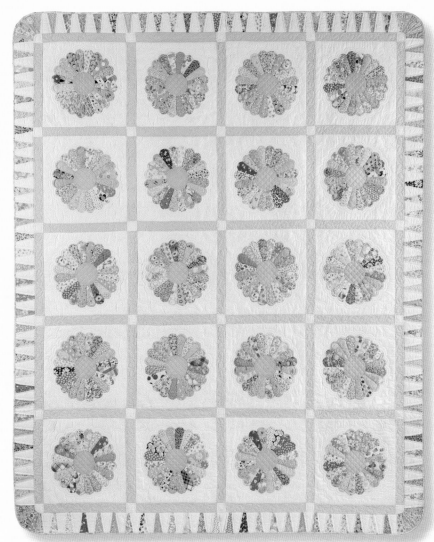

Dresden Plate Quilt, Maker Unknown.
From the collection of Terry Clothier Thompson

quilts moved into the 1930s,
floral appliqué remained popular,
although some quilters created
appliqué motifs based on beloved
animals, objects or people. One
popular dog appliqué was based
on Franklin Delano Roosevelt's
Scottish Terrier Fala.

Another unique appliqué pattern
popular in the early part of the
century was the Dresden Plate.
Although this design appeared
in quilts in earlier centuries, quilt
historians believe the 20th century
version of the motif was loosely
based on the fan design that
radiated out from the corner of a
block or border in many of the late
19th century crazy quilts. Early
Dresden Plate blocks look to be

made up of four of these fan
segments arranged to form a
circle. This motif became very well
known throughout the 1920s and
1930s. Quilts made with these
blocks grew in popularity during
the Depression, since scraps of
fabric could be used for the strips
needed to make the characteristic
circular design. These strips were
appliquéd to an inexpensive
background fabric, radiating out
from the center of the block to
form a circle. Sometimes the strips
would be pieced together into
the circle before the entire unit
was stitched to the background
fabric. The scraps used to make
the Dresden Plate blocks often
came from worn out clothing

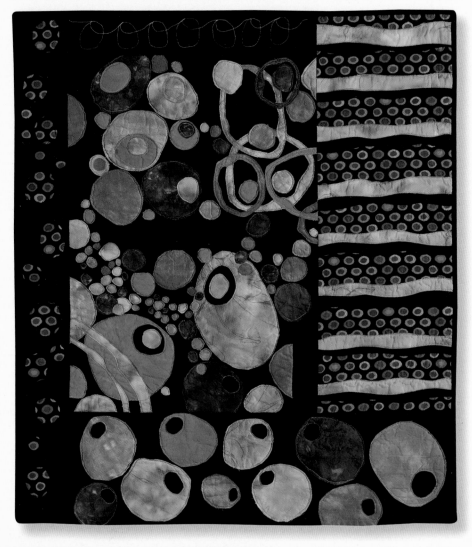

Modern Appliqué on Black Background
Olive: Color Improv. 31" x 35" Maker: Susan P. Stevenson

and feed sacks, since there was little money to purchase new fabrics for a quilt. This block was also known by other names such as Grandmother's Sunburst, Friendship Ring and Dahlia.

Quilts made for children were another early 20th century trend that included appliqué. In past centuries, children's quilts were often just miniature versions of popular patchwork designs. As early as 1910, appliqué motifs based on popular characters from children's books began to appear. The most famous of these were Sunbonnet Sue and Overall Sam. Though their

origin is not clear, some quilt historians believe these storybook characters were inspired by the illustrations of Kate Greenaway, who often drew pioneer girls with sunbonnet covered faces for outline embroidery patterns. Two women, Betty Corbett and Eulalie Osgood Grover, are thought to be responsible for the current version of the appliqué motif still used today. Their sunbonnet "babies"appeared in a popular series of children's reading primers and were soon found on many household items. Children's quilts made with the Sunbonnet Sue theme enjoyed great

popularity through the 1930s ar early 1940s before falling out of favor. The pattern enjoyed a littl revival of its own in the 1970s a has been popular ever since.

Like the Arts and Crafts movement of the late 19th and early 20th centuries, a style kno as Art Deco also influenced som quilters early in the 20th century The Art Deco style was known fo geometric shapes and straight lines, which was a move away fr the earlier colonial revival trend: of the time. This style, often fou in furniture and building design: began to influence quilt makers from the 1920s through the earl 1940s. Though most Art Deco quilts were entirely pieced, som appliqué quilt makers showed this vibe in their quilts by framir an appliquéd medallion with borders of sharp geometric shap and lines. Others would piece a geometric central design, frame with soft appliquéd vines, leaves and flowers, and then finish the quilt with sharp geometric bord There are designers today who a influenced by this style of quiltir

With the next revival later in th century, two distinctive styles of appliqué to emerge were art qui and stained glass quilts. Althoug there were earlier examples of art quilts, historians believe the modern art quilt movement beg in earnest in the 1960s, gaining in popularity through the 1970s and beyond. Many art quilters were artists in other mediums and moved to fiber art as a new outlet for their creativity. Art qui were rarely based on traditional quilt patterns. Many artists used appliqué to create their unique a imaginative designs when makir pictorial quilts, a common type art quilt. These quilts were meal to be displayed and thus were usually wall hangings and came all sizes.

Stained glass quilts emerged in the 1980s as a fun, colorful trend in quiltmaking. Quilters who made these were inspired by stained glass windows and were also influenced by architecture, much like the Art Deco quilters earlier in the century. Many of these quilts were made up of pieced colorful geometric sections framed with appliquéd thin strips of black fabric meant to mimic the glass and leading of the actual windows. Other stained glass quilts were entirely appliquéd, with the motifs stitched to a black background. The background fabric that showed between the appliqués was meant to represent the window leading.

You can see the influence of many of these 20th century styles and trends in quilts designed and made today. Floral appliqué quilting remains popular, with many designers and quilt shops offering block-of-the-month kits and classes. The fact that Marie Webster's book is still available today is another indication that this quilting style is here to stay. Traditional appliqué patterns such as the Dresden Plate continue to appear in quilts made in the 21st century and, whether you love them or not, Sunbonnet Sue block patterns are also an enduring design, especially in children's quilts. Art quilting gained popularity in the 1960s and this quilting style shows no signs of declining. The art quilt movement is still very strong, with art quilts well represented at quilt shows and in magazines. Like art quilts, stained glass quilts continue to be designed and made by many quilters today and even the Art Deco style is enjoying a recent rise in popularity.

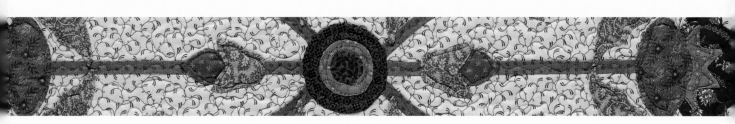

Bibliography

Classic Quilts from the American Museum in Britain, Scala Publishers, Ltd 2009 Beresford, Laura and Katherine Herbert, Curators.

Heart and Hands - Women, Quilts and American Society, Rutledge Hill Press 1987. Hedges, Elaine, Pat Ferrero and Julie Silber.

Quiltmaking in America - Beyond the Myths. Selected Writings from the American Quilt Study Group 1994, Horton, Laurel, Editor.

The American Quilt, Clarkson-Potter 1993. Kiracofe, Roderick.

Pieced by Mother. Oral Traditions Project of Union County Historical Society 1987, Lasansky, Jeannette.

Quilts in America. McGraw-Hill Book Company 1974, Orlofsky, Patsy and Myron.

The Quilt - A History and Celebration of an American Art Form. Voyageur Press 2007.Roberts, Elise Schebler.

Quilts - A Living Tradition, Hugh Lauter Levin Associates, Inc. 1995. Shaw, Robert.

Glorious American Quilts - The Quilt Collection of the Museum of American Folk Art, Penguin Studio 1996.Warren, Elizabeth V. and Sharon L. Eisenstat.

Fabric needs assume 40" of usable width for yardage, 18" x 20" of usable fabric for fat quarters and 9" x 20" of usable fabric for fat eighths.

All measurements include a ¼" seam allowance unless otherwise indicated.

STRIP SET

A strip set has two or more fabric strips that are joined together along their long sides to make one unit. Smaller segments are then cut from the strip set as needed. This is a quick way to make units for four-patch or nine-patch blocks instead of piecing individual squares

HALF-SQUARE TRIANGLE SQUARES

These are squares that are made up of two different colors. They can be made two at a time using two different colored squares cut ⅞" larger than the desired finished size of the square. For example, if your finished square is 2", the squares need to be cut 2 ⅞".

1. Cut a square from two different colors. Draw a diagonal line on the wrong side of one of the squares.

2. Layer the two squares right sides together with the marked square on top and raw edges aligned. Pin in place so the squares do not shift while stitching.

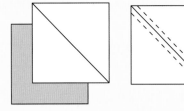

3. Sew a scant 1/4" on each side of the drawn line, then cut the squares apart on the drawn line. Press each unit open for two half-square triangle squares.

4. Trim the squares to the desired size (including seam allowance) by placing the 45-degree line of your ruler on the diagonal seam of the square. For example, if you want a 2" finished square you should measure and trim to 2 ½" (includes ¼" seam allowance all around).

FOLDED-CORNER TECHNIQUE

For some of the projects in this book, a folded-corner technique is used to add a triangle to the corner of a square. An easy and accurate way of doing this is called a folded corner. A small square is marked diagonally and sewn to the corner or corners of a larger square on the marked line. The seam is then trimmed and the block is pressed open to create a new unit.

This technique is commonly used to make Square-in-a-square units. It is also used to make flying geese units with two small squares and a rectangle.

SQUARE-IN-A-SQUARE

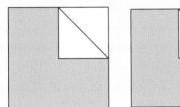 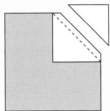 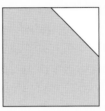

Square-in-a-square units are made up of one large square and four smaller squares. Follow the folded corner technique on all four corners of the larger square to get a unit that looks like this:

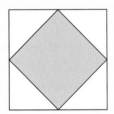

FLYING GEESE UNIT

A flying geese unit is made up of a rectangle and two squares.

Draw a diagonal line on the wrong side of the squares. Lay a square face down on the face up rectangle as shown. Sew along the drawn line. Trim the seam and press open.

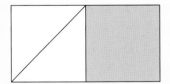 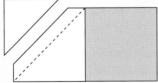 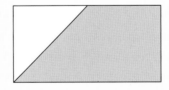

2. Repeat step 1 on the other side of the rectangle for a finished flying geese unit.

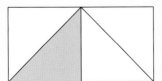 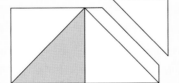 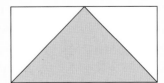

COMMON APPLIQUÉ TECHNIQUES

Appliqué quilts can be created using many different techniques and can be done by hand or machine. With so many choices available, quilters should be able to find the technique that fits their style and skill. Since there are too many types to describe here, I have chosen to highlight some of the most common methods used today.

NEEDLETURN APPLIQUÉ

This is the most traditional hand appliqué technique and has been around for centuries. It is named needleturn appliqué because the quilter uses her needle to sweep or turn under small sections of the seam allowance as she is stitching a fabric shape to the background fabric.

To begin, the appliqué shapes that make up the motif are traced onto the right side of the fabric using templates. The fabric is then cut out beyond the drawn line to add a scant ¼" seam allowance. The shapes are placed in the desired location on the background fabric (or on top of another appliqué shape if there is a motif with several layers) and held in place with pins or glue. The seam allowance is clipped to aid in shaping curves and points while turning it under with the needle. Using light cotton or silk thread that matches the color of the appliqué shape, the piece is stitched into place using a blind stitch. This is my preferred method of appliqué since it is the first technique I learned. I used needleturn appliqué to make the projects in this book. However you should use the method you are most comfortable with to make your quilts.

GENERAL HAND APPLIQUÉ

The steps for this method are similar to needleturn appliqué except that the seam allowance is turned under around the entire appliqué shape before placing it on the background fabric. Using this technique eliminates the "shape as you go" step that is needed for needleturn appliqué.

To start, the appliqué shapes are traced on to the right side of the fabric and cut out with a seam allowance (as in the needleturn method). Then the template is placed under the shape and the seam allowance is folded to the back using the template as a guide, the seam allowance is finger-pressed or ironed toward the back. Once the shape

meets the quilter's satisfaction, the template is removed, making sure the seam allowance remains turned under. Some quilters use paper templates and leave them in place while stitching. Once done, they cut away excess fabric on the back and pull out the paper template.

FREEZER PAPER APPLIQUÉ

In this method, the template is traced on the dull side of a piece of freezer paper and the shape is cut out on the line. The shape is then ironed to the right side of the piece of fabric, shiny side down, to make it stick. The shape is cut out with a 1/4" seam allowance all around. With the freezer paper still attached, the seam allowance is clipped, turned under and pressed to accurately shape the appliqué piece. Once all the seam allowance is turned under, the freezer paper is removed and the fabric shape is placed on the background using pins or glue and then stitched in place.

REVERSE APPLIQUÉ

Reverse appliqué is another hand-appliqué technique that has been around for centuries. It is thought to have originated in the 19th century with the native people who lived on the islands off the coast of Panama. However, women from Southeast Asia were also known to use this technique and carried the skill with them when they emigrated to this country. This is also about the time that Hawaiian appliqué style quilts emerged.

When doing reverse appliqué, the whole design is traced on to the background fabric instead of tracing the individual shapes on many pieces of fabric. Two or more pieces of fabric are layered and basted to the reverse side of the background fabric. The top fabric is then cut away inside the drawn line, leaving a seam allowance. Finally, the seam allowance is turned under and stitched by hand, similar to other hand appliqué methods, to create the desired shape.

The layering, cutting and stitching continues in this fashion until the whole motif is complete.

FUSIBLE MACHINE APPLIQUÉ

With the introduction of fusible products in the late 20th century, a new technique called fusible machine appliqué was developed. Since many quilters find this technique easier than hand appliqué, it has helped to sustain the popularity of appliqué quilting.

To get started, the quilter traces the appliqué shapes onto the fusible product's paper side, leaving enough space between each piece to cut out just outside the drawn line. Because the cut out shapes will be fused to the wrong side of the fabric, appliqué designs that are not symmetrical need to be traced in reverse so they will face the correct direction on the quilt top. The paper shapes are then fused by ironing them to a piece of fabric and cutting them out on the drawn line. There is no need for a seam allowance. Next the paper backing is removed and the appliqué shape is positioned and fused to the fabric using an iron. The shape is then machine-stitched around the outer edges. Typically, a small zigzag or blanket stitch and clear monofilament thread or thread matching the color of the appliqué shape is used. Some talented quilters have managed to create a machine stitching method that mimics hand appliqué. By adjusting the length and width of the hemstitch on their machine, they create a stitch that actually looks like it was done by hand.

made the projects in this book using my favorite appliqué technique, needleturn and appliqué, so I thought I would share my essential notion list and some of the tips I have picked up through the years that have made it more enjoyable. I want to pass on the joy of making quilts with appliqué to as many quilters as I can. If you love to do hand appliqué, you may know of these notions and have already used some of these tips, but some of this may be new to you.

NOTION GUIDE

There are many, many notions on the market that are made for appliqué but not all of them are absolutely necessary. Over time, you will determine which ones are important to you personally and which ones you can do without. Some of the notions I feel are the most important for a fun and relaxing hand appliqué experience are chalk marking pencils, scissors, fabric glue, appliqué pins, thread and, most importantly, the right needles.

Chalk marking pencils are used to trace around a template to draw an appliqué shape on the desired fabric. These pencils come in many varieties. Some look like regular pencils and are sharpened with a pencil sharpener. The pencil here is actually a mechanical pencil designed to hold a chalk type lead instead of regular pencil lead. I like this pencil because it makes lines that

are fine and easily erased if a mistake is made.

A small, sharp pair of scissors just for fabric is a must. I like scissors that have a serrated edge. I use these to clip into my seam allowances to aid in shaping the appliqué. Another pair of scissors just for cutting paper or cardstock templates is also needed.

I use fabric glue to hold my appliqué shapes in place for stitching. If you prefer pins, there are fine appliqué pins that will hold your shape in place but will not interfere with your stitching. I like the glue because no matter how small the pins are, I usually manage to catch my thread or prick my fingers while stitching.

To aid in hiding the hand appliqué stitch, it is important to choose the right thread. A fine thread in a color that closely matches the appliqué shape is my recommendation. I like 100% cotton threads with a silk finish. I use a 50 weight or 60 weight thread. The higher the weight number, the finer the thread. Some stitchers use 100 weight silk threads, but I have found them to be too fine and slippery for my taste.

There are many types of needles, but the ones I recommend for hand appliqué are called sharps. These are medium length needles with a sharp point and a round eye. They come in sizes 1 to 12. The larger the number, the shorter the needle. I use a size 8 or 9, but others prefer different sizes. The size you use is a personal choice based on your comfort. Some stitchers use straw needles, which are longer, thinner and more flexible than a sharp. I don't use these because I find them more difficult for stitching smaller appliqué shapes.

HANDY TIPS

GOOD LIGHTING

I find the most important factor that makes appliqué enjoyable is good lighting. No matter how good your eyesight, if the lighting in the room is dim, you will not enjoy stitching. I like to have a portable task light set up on a table or by a chair that shines light directly onto my project. The beauty of hand appliqué is small, almost invisible stitches. Working in a well–lit area helps to accomplish that. I also have a light with a built in magnifier that helps me stitch smaller appliqué pieces.

MAKING TEMPLATES

I like to use cardstock to make sturdy templates, especially if the template will be used many times. If you are unable to make a copy of your template page directly onto a piece of cardstock, you can still make cardstock templates with a few extra steps. Make a paper copy of your pattern's template page. Cut the paper templates out just outside the lines, glue them to a piece of cardstock and then cut the templates out on the lines. Now you have a cardstock backed paper template. Other materials, such as plastic or even pieces of very fine grit sand paper, can also be used.

PREPARING THE APPLIQUÉ SHAPES FOR STITCHING

Needleturn appliqué pieces are shaped by using a needle to sweep the seam allowance under the piece. Small clips in the seam allowance are needed to aid in shaping the piece. These clips need to go up to but not over the drawn line. When clipping curved parts of an appliqué piece, the more clips you have and the closer together they are, the easier it is to shape the appliqué.

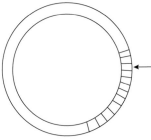

Several clips in seam
allowance
about ¼ " apart

When clipping a straight edge, fewer clips spread further apart will work just fine since a straight edge does not need much shaping. Before you begin a project, clip the seam allowances of all your pieces, that way they are ready when needed.

The most difficult things to appliqué are points. Some stitchers like their points to be very sharp.

However, since my projects tend to be on the primitive side, I don't mind if my point are a little rounded. I will use a star shape as my example. Clip the straight edges and th points as shown below.

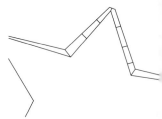

As you can see, I like to trim seam allowance a bit smaller towards the point. I also mal a clip at the top of the point and trim the seam allowance straight across. Inside corne are done in a similar fashion Clip into the seam allowance as shown, clipping up to the drawn line right in the corne

Stitch up to the point while sweeping the seam allowanc under. When you reach the point, make a stitch at the t Then rotate your project and sweep the seam allowance of the other side under, using your thumb to hold the shap in place as you sweep.

Stitch to the inside corner taking a final stitch right at corner. Then turn your proj and begin sweeping the sea allowance under and stitchi the other side.

With both points and inside corners, you may experienc a tiny fraying and have a fev threads poking out. Those be carefully clipped away a the area can be secured wit small dot of seam sealant, as FrayCheck.

LAYERING APPLIQUÉ PIECES

ome patterns have
ppliqué motifs made
p of two or more pieces
ppliquéd one on top
f another. If one piece
completely on top of
nother appliqué piece,
e smaller piece can
e stitched to the larger
ece before appliquéing
e entire motif to the
ackground. This makes
me projects easier
cause you are handling
naller sections and not
n entire quilt top. Once
smaller piece is stitched
a larger piece, cutting
vay the excess fabric
m the back, inside
e seam allowance, can
minate bulk. This is
pecially recommended
th multi-layered pieces.
can be difficult to quilt
the needle has to go
ough 4 or 5 layers of
oric.

ter the whole motif is
pliquéd to the quilt top,
e excess background
oric can also be cut
ay inside the seam
owance to relieve bulk.

CUTTING BIAS STRIPS AND MAKING STEMS

Lay your chosen fabric for
the strips flat on the cutting
surface. (Fig. A) Line up the
45-degree mark on your
ruler with the edge of the
fabric facing you. Make a
cut to start the strip. (Fig. B)
Then measure and cut the
amount of strips needed.
(Fig. C)

To make the stems, lay
a bias strip right side
down on an ironing board
and fold 1/4" in on both
lengthwise sides of the
strip. Iron to hold in place.

This will make a ½" wide
stem if you start with a 1"
strip, or ¼" wide stem if you
start with a ¾" strip. The
stems will be appliquéd on
to the quilt top with the raw
edge side down. Since there
are no seam allowances
to turn under, no clipping
is needed before stitching
down stems.

Refer to the appliqué
diagrams for each pattern
for placement of the stems.
Unless otherwise noted
in the pattern, the stems
are usually positioned and
stitched to the project first.

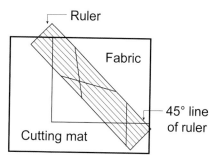

Fig. A – Ruler placement

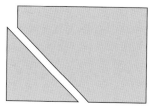

Fig. B – First 45° cut

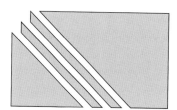

Fig. C – Cut designated
size and amount
of strips needed

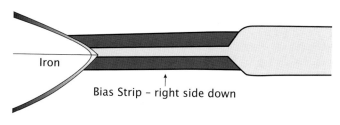

Iron

Bias Strip – right side down

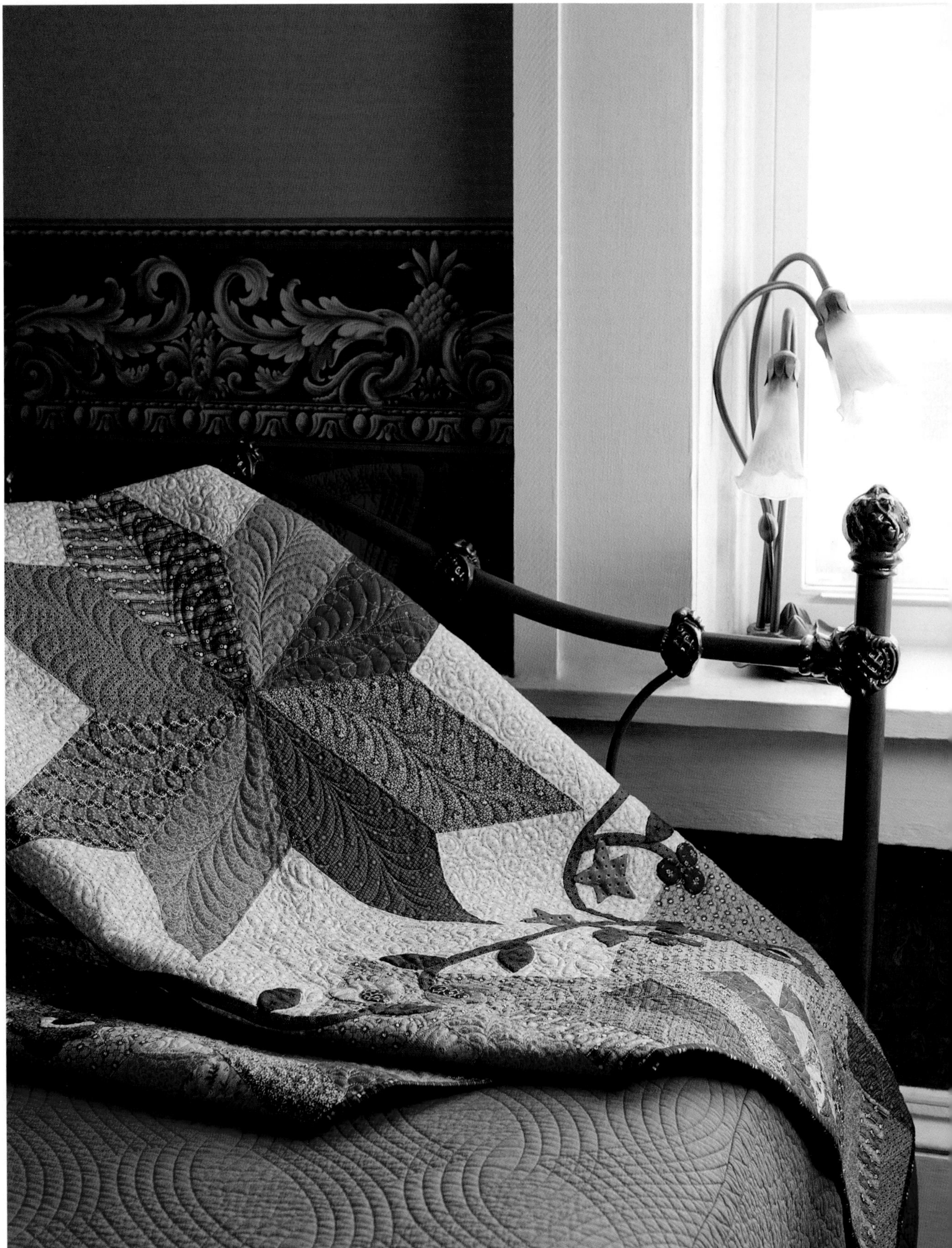

Star Gazing

FINISHED SIZE: 50 ½" square
FINISHED BLOCK SIZE: 36" square
Designed and made by Deanne Eisenman;
quilted by Annette Ashbach of
The Quiltmaker's Nest

This project was inspired by a type of Native American quilt that used a large single star as the focal point. In their culture, the star represented a connection to family members: past, present and future. The floral appliqué and the pieced border containing flying geese units is my tribute to nature, which was also important to Native Americans.

FABRICS AND MATERIALS NEEDED
FOR PIECED TOP
- 1 yard of light tan print for center star block
- 1 yard of light brown print for center star block
- 4 assorted fat eighths of medium tan prints for border flying geese units
- 8 assorted fat quarters of medium color prints for center star block and pieced border units

FOR APPLIQUÉ
- 1 - Fat quarter of dark green print #1 for stems
- 1 - 13" x 20" piece of dark green print #2 for leaves
- 1 - 5" x 6" piece of dark green print #3 for large flower calyxes
- 1 - 7" x 10" piece of medium blue print for large flowers
- 1 - 5" square piece of gold print #1 for large flowers
- 1 - 3" square piece of black print for large flowers
- 8 assorted 3" square pieces of color prints for small flowers
- 1 - 5" square piece of dark brown print for small flowers
- 1 - 9" square piece of gold print #2 for stars
- 1 - 7" x 10" piece of dark red print for berries

OTHER MATERIALS
- 56" square piece of batting and 56" square of fabric for backing
- ⅓ yard of dark blue print for binding

CUTTING INSTRUCTIONS
From the light tan print, cut:
- 4 - 6 ⅞" squares; cut diagonally once for 8 half-square triangles (B)
- 8 - 6 ½" x 12 ½" rectangles (D)
- 4 - 6 ½" squares (C)

From the light brown print, cut:
- 20 - 6 ½" squares (E)
- 2 - 1 ½" x 38 ½" inner border strips
- 2 - 1 ½" x 36 ½" inner border strips

From the assorted fat eighths medium tan prints, cut a total of:
- 72 - 2 ½" squares (G)

From the assorted fat quarters medium color prints, cut a total of:
- 8 - 6 ⅞" squares (one from each color); cut diagonally once for 16 half-square triangles (A)
- 64 - 2 ½" x 6 ½" rectangles (8 from each color) (H)
- 36 - 2 ½" x 4 ½" rectangles (4 from each of 4 colors and 5 from each of 4 colors) (F)

From the dark blue print for binding, cut:
- 6 - 1 ½" x 40" strips for single-fold binding

From the dark green print #1 for stems, cut:
- 4 - 1" x 16" bias strips
- 4 - 1" x 14" bias strips
- 8 - 1" x 5" bias strips

(See Cutting Bias Strips and Making Stems on page 23.)

ASSEMBLY INSTRUCTIONS

Refer to the layout guide on page 28 when assembling the quilt top.

CENTER STAR PANEL

1. Stack the color print A half-square triangles into 8 separate piles by color. There will be two A pieces per color. Arrange the stacks by how you want the colors to appear in your star, beginning with the top left point and moving clockwise. Label your stacks numbers 1 through 8.

2. Sew an A triangle from stack 1 to a light tan print B triangle. Press open to make a square.

3. Repeat this step with an A triangle from stacks 2 through 8, matching each with a tan B triangle. There will be a total of 4 – 6 ½" squares made up of a color triangle and a tan triangle in each square.

4. Sew a color #1 A triangle to a color #8 A triangle. Press open to make a square.

Repeat this step using the following pairs of triangles:

- a color #2 with a color # 3
- a color #4 with a color #5
- a color #6 with a color #7

There will be a total of 4 – 6 ½" squares with two different colors in each square

Lay out and join the 4 squares from step 3. Pay attention to the color number on the diagram for placement of the colors.

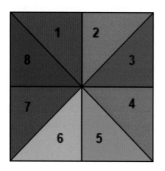

5. Join the color #1/light tan square and the color #2/light tan square from step 2.

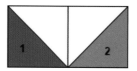

6. Repeat step 5 using colors 3 through 8 for a total of eitght color/light tan squares.

7. Join a light tan C piece to each side of the unit from step 5 to make a row. Repeat this step with the color#5/color #6 unit from step 6.

8. Lay out and join the units from steps 4 and 7, along with the remaining 2 units from step 6.

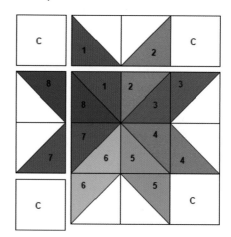

9. Using 16 light brown E pieces and 8 light tan D pieces, refer to the Flying Geese Instructions on page 19 to make 8 flying geese units measuring 6 ½" x 12 ½". There will be 4 light brown E pieces left over for later use.

10. Join 2 flying geese units from step nine to make a row. Make 4 rows.

11. Join a light brown E square to each side of a row from step 10. Make 2 rows.

12. Lay out and join the 2 rows from step 11 and the remaining 2 rows from step 10 to the center star block

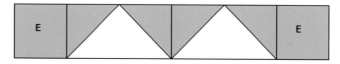

13. Join the 36 ½" inner border strips to the
    sides of the center star block. Then join
    the 38 ½" inner border strips to the top
    and bottom of the center star block.

PIECED BORDER

1. Using the 72 medium tan G pieces and
    the 36 assorted color print F pieces,
    make 36 flying geese units measuring 2
    ½" x 4 ½".

2. Join three flying geese units from step
    one into a strip. Use three different color
    geese units for a scrappy look.

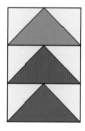

3. Repeat this step to make a total of 12
    3-piece 4 ½" x 6 ½" flying geese strips.

4. Join 2 different color H pieces on the
    long side to make a unit. The unit will
    measure 4 ½" x 6 ½". Label this unit "Unit
    1". Make a total of 2 of these units.

5. Join 4 different color H pieces on the long side into a unit. The unit will measure 8 ½" x 6 ½". Label this unit "Unit 2". Make a total of 6 of these units.

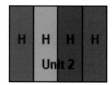

6. Join 5 different color H pieces along the long side to make a unit. The unit will measure 10 ½" x 6 ½". Label this unit "Unit 3". Make a total of 2 of these units.

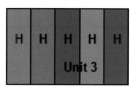

7. Join 6 different color H pieces along the long side to make a unit. The unit will measure 12 ½" x 6 ½". Label this unit "Unit 4". Make a total of 4 of these units.

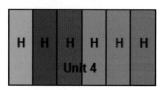

8. After making all of these units, there will be 2 different color H pieces remaining. These will be used in an upcoming step.

9. Join a Unit 1, a Unit 2, a Unit 4, three flying geese strips and an H piece into a border row. Make 2 rows.

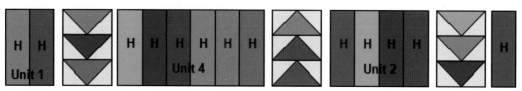

10. Join 2 Unit 2, a Unit 3, a Unit 4 and 3 flying geese strips into a border row. Make 2 rows.

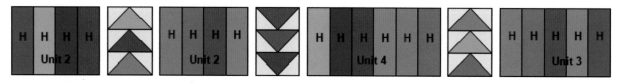

11. Join the rows from step 7 to the top and bottom of the center star panel. Flip the bottom row 180° to vary the look of the border from the top. Join the rows from step 8 to the sides of the center star panel, flipping the row on the right side 180° to vary the look from the row on the left side.

APPLIQUÉ INSTRUCTIONS

Refer to the Handy Tips on page 23 or use your preferred method of appliqué.

Appliqué templates and diagram are on pages 78 and 79.

1. Make stems from the medium green bias strips cut earlier, referring to Cutting Bias Strips and Making Stems on page 23.

2. Trace the appliqué shapes needed on the designated fabric and prepare them for stitching.

3. Position and appliqué the stems in place first. Then appliqué the large flowers, calyxes, small flowers, leaves, stars and berries in place.

FINISHING INSTRUCTIONS

1. Layer the quilt top with batting and backing.

2. Quilt as desired. Annette quilted a feather motif in the large star points and then a small overall meandering feather design over the rest of the quilt top.

3. Prepare single-fold binding with the dark blue strips cut earlier. Bind the quilt top using your preferred method.

Country Garden

FINISHED SIZE: 36 ½" square Wall Hanging
FINISHED BLOCK SIZE: 9" square
Designed, made and quilted by Deanne Eisenman

This project was inspired by the medallion appliqué quilts of the 18th and 19th centuries with a bit of a twist. The center medallion is appliquéd on a pieced background instead of on a large plain background. The pieced center is made up of two repeating blocks I call Spinning Star and Stepping Stone.

FABRICS AND MATERIALS NEEDED

FOR PIECED TOP

- 1 ⅛ yards light tan print #1 for blocks and pieced border
- ⅝ yard light tan print #2 for blocks
- 1 Fat quarter of each: medium blue #1, medium green, medium purple, medium blue #2 and medium brown prints for blocks and pieced border
- 1 Fat eighth medium red print for blocks and pieced border
- ⅓ yard dark green print for binding
- 40" square of batting and backing fabric

FOR APPLIQUÉ

- 1 Fat quarter dark green print for stems and small leaves
- 8" x 10" piece of medium green print for large leaves
- 7" piece of medium blue print for medallion center
- 9" x 14" piece dark purple for medallion center and corners
- 5" x 8" piece medium gold for medallion center and corners
- 4" x 6" piece dark blue for medallion center and corners
- 2 ½" x 3" piece dark red for medallion center and corners

- 2 assorted 4" squares of medium or dark orange prints for large flowers
- 2 assorted 4" squares of light or medium pink prints for large flowers
- 3" x 5" piece dark brown print #1 for large flowers
- 5" square medium pink print for small flowers
- 5" square medium orange print for small flowers
- 5" x 9" piece dark brown print #2 for small flowers

CUTTING INSTRUCTIONS

Label the pieces A, B, C, etc., as you cut them to avoid confusion when piecing them together.

From the light tan print #1, cut:
- 2 inner border strips 3" x 32 ½"
- 2 inner border strips 3" x 27 ½"
- 1 – 9 ½" square
- 20 – 3 ½" squares (G)
- 32 – 2 ½ x 4 ½" rectangles (J)
- 16 – 2" squares (H)

From the light tan print #2, cut:
- 16 – 3 ½" squares (D)
- 8 – 2 ⅜" squares (A)
- 112 – 2" squares (E)

From the medium blue #1 print fat quarter, cut:
- 8 – 3 ½" squares (C)
- 16 – 2 ½" squares (K)

From the medium green print fat quarter, cut:
- 8 – 3 ½" squares (C)
- 16 – 2 ½" squares (K)
- 8 – 2 " squares (F)

From the medium purple print fat quarter, cut:
- 16 – 2 ½" squares (K)
- 8 – 2 ⅜" squares (B)
- 8 – 2" squares (F)

From the medium blue #2 print fat quarter, cut:
- 8 – 3 ½" squares (I)
- 4 – 2 ½" squares (K)
- 24 – 2" squares (F)

From the medium brown print fat quarter, cut:
- 8 – 3 ½" squares (I)
- 16 – 2 ½" squares (K)
- 16 – 2" squares (F)

From the medium red print fat eighth, cut:
- 24 – 2" squares (F)

From the dark green print binding fabric, cut for single-fold binding:
- 4 – 1 ½" x 40" strips

From the dark green print #1 for stems, cut:
- 8 – 1" x 16" bias strips
- 4 – 1" x 8" bias strips

(See Cutting Bias Strips and Making Stems on page 23.)

ASSEMBLY INSTRUCTIONS

SPINNING STAR BLOCK

Refer to the General Instructions on pages 18–19 to make the following Square-in-a-square and Half-Square Triangle units.

1. Use the light tan #2 A squares and the medium purple print B squares to make 16 Half-Square Triangle units.

2. Trim the A/B units as needed to measure 2" square. Be sure to line up your ruler's 45-degree line with the center diagonal seam of this square to make sure it is trimmed evenly.

3. Lay out and join 4 units from step 2 to make a pinwheel unit that measures 3 ½" square. Repeat this step to make a total of 4 pinwheel units. Label these units Unit W.

4. Using 16 each of the purple, blue, red and brown F squares, and the light tan print #2 D squares, make 16 Square-in-a-square units that measure 3 ½" square. Do not cut off excess fabric in seam allowance until the entire unit is finished and measured. Label these squares Unit X.

Set aside the remaining purple, blue and red F squares for later use in the Stepping Stone block instructions.

5. Draw a diagonal line on the wrong side of the light tan print #2 E pieces. Set aside 48 of these pieces for the Stepping Stone blocks. Using 32 light tan print #2 E squares and 8 blue print #1 C squares, make 16 Square-in-a-square units that measure 3 ½" square. Do not cut off excess fabric in seam allowance until the entire unit is finished and measured. Label these squares Unit Y.

6. Repeat step 5 with the 8 green print C squares and 32 light tan print #2 E squares to make 8 units that measure 3 ½". Label these squares Unit Z.

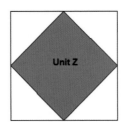

7. Join a Unit X, a Unit Y and a Unit Z into a row that measures 3 ½" x 9 ½". Make a total of 8 rows. Pay attention to the how the color corners are rotated on Unit X. It's important to assemble the row exactly as pictured to create the spinning star design.

8. Sew a Unit X to each side of a Unit W to make a row that measures 3 ½" x 9 ½". Make a total of 4 rows. Once again, pay attention to the direction of the color corners on the Unit X.

9. Join 2 rows from step 7 and 1 row from step 8 to construct a Spinning Star block. The block should measure 9 ½". Like the row construction, pay attention to the color placement when joining the rows. Repeat this step to make a total of 4 blocks.

Set these blocks aside for the Quilt Top Assembly.

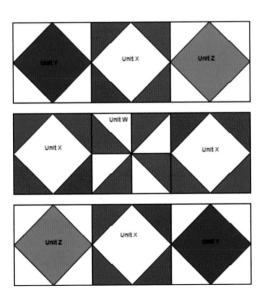

STEPPING STONE BLOCK

Before beginning, set aside 4 light tan print #1 G squares for later.

1. Draw a diagonal line on the wrong side of the light tan print #1 H squares. These will be used in upcoming steps along with the 48 light tan #2 E squares set aside earlier.

2. Take 24 light tan print #2 E squares, 8 light tan print #1 H squares, and 8 blue print #2 I squares to make 8 Square-in-a-square units measuring 3 1/2". Each unit will have 3 light tan print #2 corners and 1 light tan print #1 corner. Do not cut off excess fabric in seam allowance until the entire unit is finished and measured. Label these squares Unit Y.

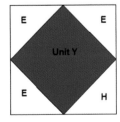

3. Repeat step 2 with the remaining light tan print #1 H squares, light tan print #2 E squares and the brown print I squares to make 8 units that measure 3 ½" square. Label these squares Unit Z.

4. Draw a diagonal line on the wrong side of the green print F squares. These will be used in upcoming steps along with the purple print, blue print #2 and red print F squares set aside earlier. Using 8 purple F squares, 8 green F squares and 8 light tan print #1 G squares, refer to the Folded-Corner Technique on page 19 of General Instructions to make a total of 8 "half" Square-in-a-square units that measures 3 ½". Do not cut off excess fabric in the seam allowance until the entire unit is finished and measured. Label these squares Unit W.

5. Repeat step 4 with the 8 red F squares, 8 blue F squares and 8 light tan print #1 G squares. Make a total of 8 "half" Square-in-a-square units that measure 3 ½". Label these squares Unit X.

6. Sew a Unit X, Y and Z into a row. Pay attention to the positioning of the Y and Z units so the light tan print #1 H corner is pointing in towards the center of the row. This row will measure 3 ½" x 9 ½". Make a total of 8 rows.

7. Join two Unit W units and a light tan print #1 G piece into a row. This row will measure 3 ½" x 9 ½". Make a total of 4 rows.

8. Join 2 rows from step 6 and 1 row from step 7 to construct a Stepping Stone block. Pay attention to the color placement in the diagram for positioning of the rows. The block should measure 9 ½" square. Make a total of 4 blocks.

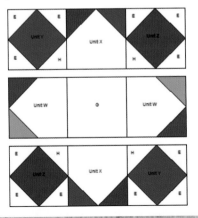

CENTER PANEL ASSEMBLY

1. Join 2 Spinning Star blocks and 1 Stepping Stone block into a row that measures 9 ½" x 27 ½". Make 2 rows.

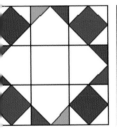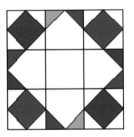

2. Join 2 Stepping Stone blocks and the light tan print #1 9 ½" square cut earlier into a row that measures 9 ½" x 27 ½". Make 1 row

3. Join the rows from steps 1 and 2 to construct the center panel. It should measure 27 ½".

4. Sew the 27 ½" inner border strips to the sides of the center panel. Then sew the 32 ½" inner border strips to the top and bottom of the center panel.

PIECED OUTER BORDER

Refer to the General Instructions on page 19 for making the following Flying Geese units.

1. Draw a diagonal line on the wrong side of the blue print #1, green print, purple print, and brown print K squares. Use 16 blue print #1 K squares and 8 light tan print #1 J rectangles to make 8 blue/tan flying geese units that measure 2 ½" x 4 ½".

2. Repeat step 1 with the green, purple and brown K squares, and the remaining light tan print #1 J rectangles. There will be a total of 8 green/tan, 8 purple/tan and 8 brown/tan flying geese units that measure 2 ½ x 4 ½".

3. Join 2 of each color flying geese units from steps 1 and 2 into a row, alternating the colors to keep a scrappy look. Make 4 rows that measure 2 ½" x 32 ½".

4. Sew a blue print #2 K piece to each end of 2 of the flying geese rows from step 3.

5. Sew a row from step 3 to each side of the center panel and then sew a row from step 4 to the top and bottom of the center panel to finish piecing the wall hanging.

APPLIQUÉ INSTRUCTIONS

Refer to the Handy Tips on page 23 or use your preferred method of appliqué. Appliqué templates and diagram are on pages 80–82.

1. Join 2 of the dark green 16" bias strips at the ends to make a 32" bias strip. Repeat this step with the other six 16" bias strips to make a total of four 32" bias strips. To make stems from these and the dark green 8" bias strips, refer to Cutting Bias Strips and Making Stems on page 23.

2. Trace the appliqué shapes needed onto the designated fabric and prepare them for stitching.

3. Referring to the diagram, position and appliqué the stems in place first. The 32" stems will span across each side of the inner border and the 8" stems will radiate from the center of the plain block in the middle. Then position and appliqué the center large leaves, medallion piece, large flowers and small leaves. Finally, position and appliqué the corner medallion pieces, the small flowers and small leaves in the border.

FINISHING INSTRUCTIONS

1. Layer the quilt top with batting and backing.

2. Quilt as desired. I quilted a free hand design in the pieced blocks, echo quilting inside the appliqués and did a free motion meandering in the plain space.

3. Prepare single-fold binding with the dark green strips cut earlier. Bind the quilt top using your preferred method.

Summer Evening Blooms

FINISHED SIZE: 44 ½" square
FINISHED BLOCK Size: 12" square
Designed and made by Deanne Eisenman; quilted by Jean Miller of Prairie Sun Quilting

Ideas for a quilt can come from many places and Summer Evening Blooms is the result of combining the ideas that sparked my imagination. For this quilt, the inspiration came from the look of flowers dangling from a hanging basket as the sun was setting and an Evening Star block I spied in an antique quilt. Putting the two ideas together led me to this design.

FABRIC AND MATERIALS NEEDED

FOR PIECED TOP

- ⅝ yard medium tan print for setting strip blocks and inner border
- ⅜ yard light tan #1 print for Summer Star blocks
- ¼ yard light tan #2 print for Summer Star blocks
- ½ yard dark blue #1 print for stars in Summer Star blocks
- 1 Fat quarter dark blue #2 print for four-patch units in Summer Star blocks
- 6 assorted fat quarters of medium/light color prints for both blocks and out pieced border
- 52" square piece of batting and backing fabric
- ¼ yard dark green print for binding

FOR APPLIQUÉ

- 1 Fat eighth dark green for stems
- 12" square piece of dark green print for leaves
- 8" square piece of dark brown #1 print for large flower
- 4 assorted light color print 3" squares for large flowers
- 8 assorted medium color print 2 ½" squares for large flowers
- 8 assorted dark color print 1 ½" squares for large flowers
- 6 assorted medium/light color print 3" x 6" pieces for small flowers
- 5" x 6" piece of dark brown #2 print for small flowers
- 5" x 6" piece of dark red for berries

CUTTING INSTRUCTIONS

From the medium tan print, cut:
- 2 – 2 ½" x 36 ½" inner border strips
- 4 – 2 ½" x 20 ½" inner border strips
- 16 – 2 ½" x 4 ½" rectangles (L)
- 16 – 2 ½" squares (N)

From the light tan #1 print, cut:
- 40 – 2" x 3 ½" rectangles (E)
- 40 – 2" squares (G)

From the light tan #2 print, cut:
- 20 – 3 ½" squares (J)

From the dark blue #1 print, cut:
- 80 – 2" squares (F)
- 40 – 1 ¼" x 2" rectangles (B)
- 40 – 1 ¼" squares (D)

From the dark blue #2 print, cut:
- 6 – 2" x 20" strips (H)

From each of the 6 assorted medium/light color fat quarters, cut:
- 1 – 2" x 20" strips for a total of 6 strips (I)

From each of 2 of the assorted medium/light color fat quarters, fat quarters, cut:
- 2 – 2" squares for a total of 2 squares (A)
- 8 – 1 ¼" squares for a total of 16 squares (C)

From each of the other 4 assorted medium/light color fat quarters, cut:
- 2 – 2" squares for a total of 8 squares (A)
- 16 – 1 ¼" squares for a total of 64 squares (C)

From the remaining fabric from the 6 fat quarters cut a total of:
- 8 – 2 ½" x 12 ½" rectangles (O) for setting strip blocks
- 8 – 2 ½" x 8 ½" rectangles (M) for setting strip blocks
- 8 – 2 ½" x 4 ½" rectangles (K) for setting strip blocks
- 84 – 2 ½" squares (P) for the pieced outer border

From the dark green print binding fabric, cut:
- 5 – 1 ½" x 40" strips for single-fold binding

For the stems, from the dark green, cut:
- 8 – ¾" x 12 ½" bias strips
- 4 – ¾" x 3" bias strips

(See Cutting Bias Strips and Making Stems on page 23.)

ASSEMBLY INSTRUCTIONS
SUMMER STAR BLOCK

1. Draw a diagonal line on the wrong side of the assorted color print C pieces. Using these C pieces and the dark blue print # 1 B pieces, refer to the Flying Geese Instructions on page 19 of General Instructions to make 40 flying geese that measure 1 ¼" x 2".

2. Lay out and join 4 flying geese units from step 1 with a matching color A piece and 4 dark blue #1 print D pieces to construct a small star measuring 3 ½". Make a total of 10 small stars.

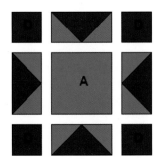

3. Make flying geese units using the light tan #1 print E pieces and the dark blue #1 print F pieces. Make a total of 40 flying geese units that measure 2" x 3 ½".

4. Lay out and join a small star unit from step 2, 4 of the flying geese units from step 3 and 4 light tan #1 print G pieces to make a star unit for this block. This unit should measure 6 ½" square. Make a total of 10 units.

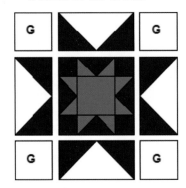

5. Using a dark blue #2 H strip and a color print I strip, refer to the Strip Set Instructions on page 18 to make a total of 6 strips sets that measure 3 ½" x 20".

6. Cross cut segments from these strips sets that measure 2" x 3 ½". Cut a total of 40 segments.

7. Join 2 segments (with different color I pieces) from step 6 to make a four-patch unit measuring 3 ½".

8. Lay out and join 2 four-patch units (with different color I pieces) from step 7 and 2 light tan #2 print J pieces to make a checkerboard unit for this block. Make a total of 10 units that measure 6 ½".

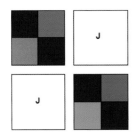

9. Lay out and join 2 star units from step 4 and 2 checkerboard units from step 8 to make a Summer Star block that measures 12 ½". The star units used should have 2 different color center stars. Make a total of 5 Summer Star blocks.

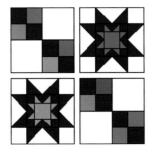

SETTING STRIP BLOCKS

1. Sew a medium tan print L piece to each side of a color print K piece to make a row. Make 8 rows that measure 2 ½" x 12 ½".

2. Sew a medium tan print N piece to each side of a color print M piece to make a row. Make 8 rows that measure 2 ½" x 12 ½".

3. Lay out and join 2 rows from step 1, 2 rows from step 2 and 2 color print O pieces to make a setting strip block. Choose the rows and O pieces for each block so you do not have colors that are the same right next to each other, but the same color can appear in the block more than once. Make a total of 4 setting strip blocks that measure 12 ½" square.

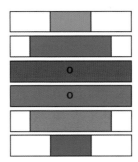

CENTER PANEL ASSEMBLY

1. Lay out and join 2 Summer Star blocks and a setting strip block into a row. Make 2 rows.

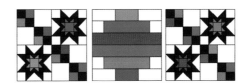

2. Lay out and join 2 setting strip blocks and a Summer Star block into a row. Note that the setting strip blocks are rotated 90° from the one in the rows from step 1. Make 1 row.

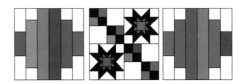

3. Lay out and join the rows from steps 1 and 2 to make the center panel. This should measure 36 ½" square.

4. Join 2 of the 20 ½" medium tan print inner border strips at the ends to make a 40 ½" long strip. Make 2.

5. Sew the medium tan print 36 ½" inner border strips to the sides of the center panel. Then sew the medium tan print 40 ½" inner border strips to the top and bottom of the center panel.

PIECED OUTER BORDER

Make sure to use a random mix of the colored border P squares when piecing the border rows to make them scrappy.

1. Join 20 P squares to make a row. Make 2 rows that measure 40 ½" long.

2. Join 22 P squares to make a row. Make 2 rows that measure 44 ½" long.

3. Sew the 40 ½" outer border rows to the sides of the center panel. Then sew the 44 ½" outer border rows to the top and the bottom of the center panel.

APPLIQUÉ INSTRUCTIONS

Refer to the Handy Tips on page 23 or use your preferred method of appliqué.

Appliqué templates and diagram are on page 83 and 84.

1. Join 2 of the dark green 12 ½" bias strips at the ends to make a 24 ½" bias strip. Repeat this step with the other six 12 ½" bias strips to make a total of four 24 ½" bias strips. To make stems from these and the dark green 3" bias strips, refer to Cutting Bias Strips and Making Stems on page 23.

2. Trace the appliqué shapes needed on the designated fabric and prepare them for stitching.

3. Position and appliqué the stems in place referring to the diagram. The 24 ½" stems will spiral inside the setting strip blocks and the three 3" stems will radiate out from those longer stems.

4. Position and appliqué the large flowers, small flowers, leaves and berries.

The appliqué diagram shows only one setting strip block. All four blocks are appliquéd in the same manner.

FINISHING INSTRUCTIONS

1. Layer the quilt top with batting and backing.

2. Quilt as desired. Jean Miller quilted a free motion flower motif in the Summer Star blocks and echo quilted the appliqué in the setting strip blocks to fill in the space. The borders have a large meandering loops and stars motif.

3. Prepare single-fold binding with the dark green strips cut earlier. Bind the quilt top using your preferred method.

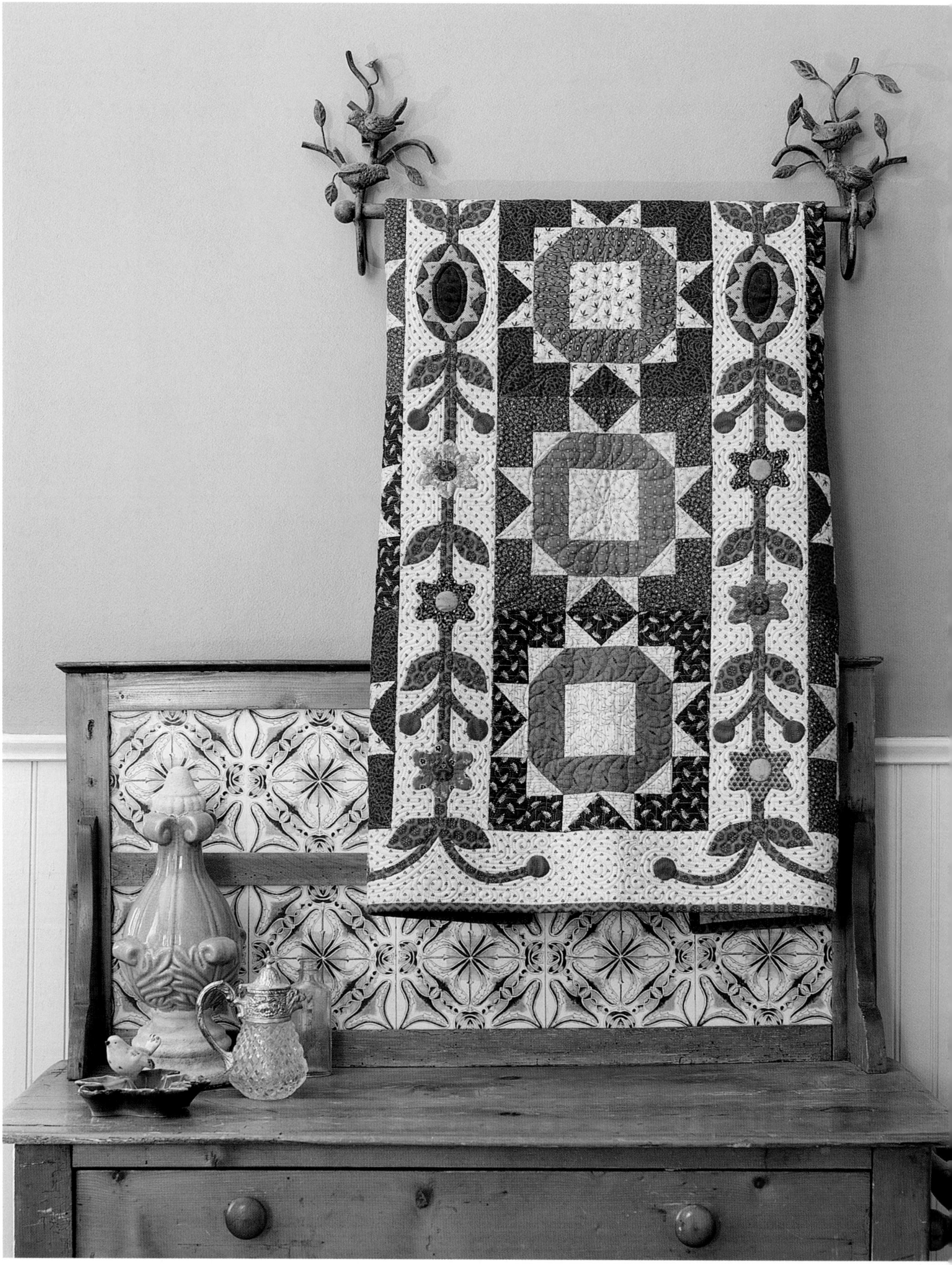

Open Windows

FINISHED SIZE: 35 ½" x 51 ½" Wall Hanging
FINISHED BLOCK SIZE: 9" square

Designed and made by Deanne Eisenman; quilted by Jean Miller of Prairie Sun Quilting.

This quilt was inspired by the friendship or autograph quilts of the mid–19th century with a little twist, of course. I set my blocks in columns with a plain border strip separating them so I could add appliqué embellishment, which was not common among these quilts. The centers of the pieced blocks are meant for signatures or verses to be passed along to a friend leaving a group or a community.

FABRIC AND MATERIALS NEEDED

FOR PIECED TOP
- ⅞ yard light tan #1 print for inner and outer border strips
- 3 assorted ⅓ yard pieces of light tan #2 prints for blocks
- 3 assorted ⅓ yard pieces of dark color prints for blocks
- 3 assorted ¼ yard pieces of medium color prints for blocks
- 43" x 57" piece of batting and backing fabric
- ¼ yard dark green print for binding

FOR APPLIQUÉ
- 1 Fat quarter dark green print for stems and leaves
- 5" x 7" piece of medium purple print for center medallions
- 5" x 7" piece of light gold print for center medallions
- 3¼" x 4" piece of dark blue print for center medallions
- 8 assorted 3" square pieces of medium color prints for flowers
- 8 assorted 3" square pieces of dark color prints for flowers
- 6" square piece dark brown print for flowers
- 6" square piece medium gold print for flowers
- 6" x 12" piece dark red print for berries

CUTTING INSTRUCTIONS

From the light tan #1 print, cut:
- 4 – 4 ½" x 23" border strips
- 2 – 3 ½" x 35 ½" border strips

From each of the light tan #2 prints, cut:
- 5 – 3 ½" squares (A) for a total of 15
- 10 – 2 ⅜" squares (D) for a total of 30
- 40 – 2" squares (F) for a total of 120

From each of the dark color prints, cut:
- 40 – 2" x 3 ½" rectangles (E) for a total of 120
- 20 – 2" squares (G) for a total of 60

From each of the medium color prints, cut:
- 10 – 2 ⅜" squares (C) for a total of 30
- 20 – 2" x 3 ½" rectangles (B) for a total of 60

From the dark green binding fabric, cut:
- 5 – 1 ½" x 40" strips for single–fold binding

From the dark green fabric for stems and leaves, cut:
- 4 – 1" x 22 ½" bias strips
- 2 – ¾" x 16" bias strips
- 4 – ¾" x 9" bias strips
- 4 – ¾" x 5" bias strips

(See Cutting Bias Strips and Making Stems on page 23.)

ASSEMBLY INSTRUCTIONS

OPEN WINDOW BLOCK

Each block will be made up of 1 dark color print, 1 medium color print and 1 light tan #2 print. Keep this in mind when piecing the individual sections of the blocks.

1. Using the light tan #2 print D squares and the assorted medium print C squares, refer to the Half-Square Triangle squares instructions on page 18 to make a total of 60 half-square triangle squares.

Trim the units as needed to measure 2". Be sure to line up your ruler's 45-degree line with the center diagonal seam of the square to make sure it is trimmed evenly.

2. Join 2 matching color triangle squares from step 1 to each side of a matching color medium print B rectangle to make a row. Make 2 rows that measure 2" x 6 ½".

3. Join 2 medium color print B rectangles (the same color as used in step 2) to each side of a light tan #2 print A square. Make 1 row that measures 3 ½" x 6 ½".

4. Join the rows from steps 2 and 3 to make the center of the block. This unit should measure 6 ½".

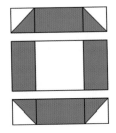

Repeat steps 2 through 4 to make a total of 15 of these center units.

Set aside 60 dark color print E rectangles (20 from each color) for a later step.

5. Using the light tan #2 print F squares and the remaining assorted color print E rectangles, refer to the Flying Geese instructions on page 19 to make 60 flying geese units that measure 2" x 3 ½".

6. Join matching dark color print G squares to each side of a flying geese unit of the same color to make a row. Make 2 rows that measure 2" x 6 ½".

7. Join matching dark color print E pieces to each side of a flying geese unit of the same color to make a row. Make 2 rows that measure 2" x 9 ½".

8. Join a row from step 6 to each side of a center unit. Then join a row from step 7 to the top and bottom of the unit to complete the Open Window block. The block will measure 9 ½".

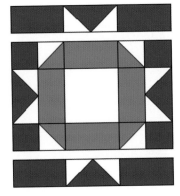

Repeat steps 6 through 8 to make a total of 15 Open Window blocks.

QUILT TOP ASSEMBLY

1. Join 5 Open Window blocks into a row. Alternate the colors so each row is different and will make the quilt scrappier. Using a design wall or large floor space during this step is helpful in planning your color placement. Make 3 rows.

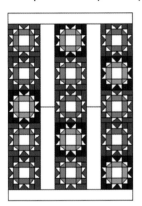

2. Join 2 of the 4 ½" x 23" light tan #1 border strips at the ends to make one 45 ½" long strip. Make 2.

3. Lay out and join the Open Window block rows and the 2 inner border strips from step 2. Then join the light tan #1 print border strips to the top and the bottom to complete the quilt top.

APPLIQUÉ INSTRUCTIONS

Appliqué templates are on page 85.

1. Join together 2 of the dark green 22 ½" bias strips at the ends to make a 44 ½" bias strip. Make 2. Make stems from these and the dark green 16", 9" and 5" bias strips, referring to Cutting Bias Strips and Making Stems on page 23.

2. Cut the two 16" stems in to 16 - 2" stems. These will be used as the berry stems.

3. Trace the appliqué shapes needed onto the designated fabric and prepare them for stitching.

4. Position and appliqué the stems in place first referring to the diagram. The 44 ½" stems will be in the center of each light tan #1 print inner border. The 9" and 5" stems will be stitched on the ends of these long stems radiating out into the upper and lower borders.

5. Position and appliqué the center medallions, flowers, leaves and berries.

The top and bottom of the quilt are mirror images, the diagram just shows the top portion of the quilt.

FINISHING INSTRUCTIONS

1. Layer the quilt top with batting and backing.

2. Quilt as desired. Jean Miller quilted a free motion flower and loop motif in the Open Window blocks and echo quilted the appliqué in the borders to fill in the space.

3. Prepare single-fold binding with the dark green strips cut earlier. Bind the quilt top using your preferred method.

Pathways Lap Quilt

FINISHED SIZE: 66 ½" square
FINISHED BLOCK SIZE: 12" square
Designed and made by Deanne Eisenman; quilted by Annette Ashbach of The Quiltmaker's Nest.

Pathways is my tribute to the shift away from medallion quilts in the mid 19th century to the more uniform, block style quilts. Many of these quilts featured a center made up of repeating blocks, an appliquéd inner border and a pieced outer border. My version has more of a scrappy look than those older quilts since I used twelve different colors of fabrics, something not common in that century.

FABRIC AND MATERIALS NEEDED

When picking your fabric for this quilt, choose dark colors and medium colors that coordinate well in groups of three. The tan fabrics can be light or medium or both, your choice. Before cutting, you will be instructed to separate fabrics into 4 color sets, each containing 3 color print fabrics and 3 tan print fabrics. Each color set of fabrics will produce 4 Pathway Star blocks, 2 with a color print background (Block Y) and 2 with a tan print background (Block Z). The key to successful piecing is to carefully label the pieces as you cut and keep them in their separate color sets, and further separated by Block Y or Block Z. The piecing instructions for the blocks are simple so once you have your fabric separated and cut, the blocks should go together quickly. Good organization is required!

FOR THE PIECED TOP:

- 3 assorted ½ yard tan prints for inner appliqué border

For the blocks and pieced outer border:
- ⅓ yard pieces of each: dark green, dark purple, dark red #1 and dark brown prints
- ½ yard pieces of each: dark red #2 and dark blue prints
- ⅓ yard pieces of each: medium purple, medium green, medium orange and medium blue prints
- ½ yard pieces of each: medium pink and medium gold prints
- 8 assorted ⅓ yard pieces of tan prints
- 4 assorted ½ yard pieces of different tan prints

FOR APPLIQUÉ

- ½ yard medium green #1 print for stems
- 1 Fat Quarter (⅓ yard) medium green #2 print for leaves
- 1 – 6" x 9" piece dark red #1 for large flowers
- 1 – 4" x 6" piece medium gold for large flowers
- 1 – 4" x 8" piece medium brown for large flower calyxes
- 10 assorted 2" x 4" pieces of various color prints for small flowers
- 1 – 8" x 10" piece medium green #3 for small flower calyxes
- 1 – 8" x 9" piece dark red #2 for berries

OTHER MATERIALS

- 78" square piece of batting and backing fabric
- ½ yard dark green print for double-fold binding

SEPARATING FABRICS

Separate the fabrics into 4 color sets as indicated below. Be sure to also label the fabrics within the sets as indicated.

Color Set 1
Dark green print (color #1)
Dark purple print (color #2)
Dark red #2 print (color #3)
2 assorted ½ yard pieces of tan print (tan #1 & tan #2)
⅓ yard tan print (tan #3)

Color Set 2
Dark red #1print (color #1)
Dark brown print (color #2)
Dark blue print (color #3)
2 assorted ⅓ yard pieces of tan print (tan #1 & tan #2)
½ yard tan print (tan #3)

Color Set 3
Medium purple print (color #1)
Medium green print (color #2)
Medium pink print (color #3)
2 assorted ⅓ yard pieces of tan print (tan #1 & tan #2)
½ yard tan print (tan #3)

Color Set 4
Medium orange print (color #1)
Medium blue print (color #2)
Medium gold print (color #3)
2 assorted ⅓ yard pieces of tan print (tan #1 & tan #2)
½ yard tan print (tan #3)

CUTTING INSTRUCTIONS

Cut your fabrics in the order given:
1) Outer Pieced Border
2) Inner Appliqué Border
3) Blocks

All measurements include a ¼" seam allowance unless otherwise indicated.

OUTER PIECED BORDER

The fabric from the color sets will be used. Be sure to return each fabric to its color set after cutting.

From each of 3 of the dark color prints from color set #1 and 3 of the medium color prints from color set #3, cut:

- 3 – 3 ⅞" squares for a total of 18 squares

From each of the 3 dark color prints from color set #2 and the 3 medium color prints from color set #4, cut:

- 4 – 3 ⅞" squares for a total of 24 squares

From 6 of the tan prints, cut:

- 3 – 3 ⅞" squares for a total of 18 squares

From the other 6 tan prints, cut:

- 4 – 3 ⅞" squares for a total of 24 squares

Set these pieces aside for the Outer Pieced Border section beginning on page 54.

INNER APPLIQUÉ BORDER

From each of the 3 assorted tan prints, cut:

- 12 – 6 ½" squares for a total of 36 squares

From the medium green #1 print, cut:
- 12 – 1" x 18" bias strips
- 20 – 1" x 5 ½" bias strips
- 4 – 1" x 4 ½" bias strips

(See Cutting Bias Strips and Making Stems on page 23.)

PATHWAY STAR BLOCKS

The following instructions are for one set of fabric. Repeat the instructions below for all 4 sets.

Label the pieces using the alphabet characters in the instructions. The first letter in the parenthesis stands for the piece in the block and the second letter stands for the block. For example: B–Y means piece B for block Y and D–Z means piece D for block Z.

From color print #1, cut:
- 8 – 2 ½" squares (B–Y)
- 16 – 2 ½" squares (D–Z)

From color print #2, cut:
- 8 – 2 ½" x 4 ½" rectangles (C–Y)
- 8 – 2 ½" squares (E–Y)
- 16 – 2 ½" squares (D–Z)

From color print #3, cut:
- 2 – 4 ½" squares (A–Z)
- 8 – 2 ½" x 8 ½" rectangles (F–Y)
- 8 – 2 ½" squares (E–Y)

From tan print #1, cut:
- 2 – 4 ½" squares (A–Y)
- 8 – 2 ½" squares (B–Z)

From tan print #2, cut:
- 8 – 2 ½" x 4 ½" rectangles (C–Z)
- 16 – 2 ½" squares (D–Y)
- 8 – 2 ½" squares (E–Z)

From tan print #3, cut:
- 8 – 2 ½" x 8 ½" rectangles (F–Z)
- 16 – 2 ½" squares (D–Y)
- 8 – 2 ½" squares (E–Z)

BINDING

From the dark green print, cut:
- 7 – 2 ½" x 40" strips for double–fold binding

ASSEMBLY INSTRUCTIONS

PATHWAY STARS – BLOCK Y

Each color set will make 2 of Block Y, for a total of 8 Block Ys, each measuring 12 ½" square.

The following instructions are for one Block Y. Repeat these steps to make all 8 blocks.

1. Using 4 color print #1 B–Y pieces from 4 different color sets and a tan print #1 A–Y piece, refer to the Square–in–a–square Instructions on page 19 to make 1 – 4 ½" square. Do not cut off excess fabric in seam allowance until the entire unit is finished and measured.

2. Using 8 tan print #2 D–Y pieces and 4 color print #2 C–Y pieces, refer to the Flying Geese Instructions on page 19 to make 4 flying geese units that measure 2 ½" x 4 ½".

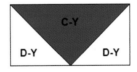

3. Sew a color print #3 E–Y square to each side of a flying geese unit from the previous step to make a row that measures 2 ½" x 8 ½". Make 2 rows.

4. Lay out and join the square from step 1, the rows from step 3 and the 2 other flying geese units to construct the center of the block that measures 8 ½" square.

5. Using 8 tan print #3 D–Y pieces and 4 color print #3 F–Y pieces, refer to the Folded Corner Technique Instructions on page 19 to make 4 units that measure 2 ½" x 8 ½".

6. Sew a color print #2 E–Y piece to each side of the unit from step 5 to make a row that measures 2 ½" x 12 ½". Make 2 rows.

7. Lay out and join the center of the block constructed previously, the 2 rows from step 6 and the remaining 2 units from step 5 to finish the Pathway Star – Block Y. The block should measure 12 ½" square.

PATHWAY STARS – BLOCK Z

Each color set will make 2 of Block Z, for a total of 8 that measure 12 ½" square.

The following instructions are for one Block Z. Repeat the following steps to make all 8 blocks.

1. Follow step 1 of the Block Y instructions to make a center square-in-a square unit from 1 color print #3 A–Z piece and 4 tan print #1 B–Z pieces.

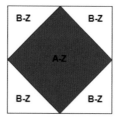

2. Follow step 2 of the Block Y instructions to make 4 flying geese units using the tan print #2 C–Z and the color print #2 D–Z pieces.

3. Follow step 3 of the Block Y instructions using 2 flying geese units from step 2 and the tan print #3 E–Z pieces to make the rows for the center of the block.

4. Follow step 4 of the Block Y instructions to make the center unit of the Block Z.

5. Follow step 5 of the Block Y instructions using the tan print #3 F–Z and the color print #1 D–Z pieces to make the 4 units.

6. Follow step 6 of the Block Y instructions using the units made in step 5 and the tan print #2 E–Z pieces to make 2 rows.

7. Follow the last step of the Block Y instructions to complete Block Z.

8. There should now be a total of 16 blocks, each measuring 12 ½" square: 8 of Block Y and 8 of Block Z.

QUILT TOP ASSEMBLY

Before making the rows in the instructions below, you may want to lay out all 16 blocks into 4 rows of 4 blocks each, alternating between Block Y and Block Z in the rows. This will help you achieve the color placement that you want.

1. Join 2 Block Y and 2 Block Z into a row. Make 2 rows that measure 12 ½" x 48 ½".

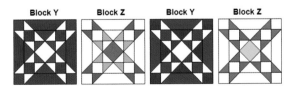

2. Join 2 Block Y and 2 Block Z into a row. Make 2 rows that measure 12 ½" x 48 ½".

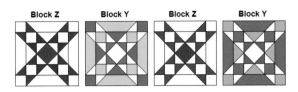

3. Join the 4 rows constructed in steps 1 and 2 to make the center of the quilt top.

INNER PIECED APPLIQUÉ BORDER

1. Join 8 of the inner border tan print 6 ½" squares into a row. Alternate between the different tan prints to make the row scrappy. Make 2 rows that measure 6 ½" x 48 ½".

2. Repeat step 1 with 10 inner border tan print 6 ½" squares. Make 2 rows that measure 6 ½" x 60 ½".

3. Sew the rows from step 1 to the sides of the quilt, then sew the rows from step 2 to the top and bottom of the quilt.

PIECED OUTER BORDER

1. Referring to the Half-Square Triangle Instructions on page 19, use the assorted tan print and assorted color print 3 ⅞" squares to make 84 half-square triangle units.

2. Trim the squares from step 1 as needed to measure 3 ½" square. Be sure to line up your ruler's 45 degree line with the center diagonal seam of this square to make sure it is trimmed evenly.

3. This is another spot in this project where you want to plan color placement as the squares from this step are joined into rows for the borders. Join 20 squares into a row measuring 3 ½" x 60 ½". Make 2 rows.

Row of 20 squares

4. Repeat step 3 with 22 squares. Make 2 rows measuring 3 ½" x 66 ½". Take note of the direction of the last square in these 2 rows. This makes the pattern as seen in the photo.

Row of 22 squares   last square

5. Sew the rows from step 3 to the sides of the quilt, then sew the rows from step 4 to the top and the bottom.

APPLIQUÉ INSTRUCTIONS

Appliqué templates and diagrams are on page 88 and 89.

1. Join 3 of the medium green #1 print 18" bias strips at the ends to make a 52" bias strip. Repeat this step with the other nine 18" bias strips for a total of 4 – 52" bias strips. Make stems from these and the medium green #1 print 5 ½" and 4 ½" bias strips, referring to Cutting Bias Strips and Making Stems on page 23.

2. Trace the appliqué shapes needed onto the designated fabrics and prepare them for stitching.

3. Position and appliqué the stems in place first. The 52" stems will gently wave inside the inner borders from corner to corner. The 5 ½" stems will radiate out from those long stems on the sides for the small flowers. The 4 ½" stems will extend from the four corners for the large flowers.

4. Position and appliqué the large flowers, small flowers, calyxes, leaves and berries.

FINISHING INSTRUCTIONS

1. Layer the quilt top with batting and backing.

2. Quilt as desired. Annette Ashbach quilted a free motion feather motif in the Pathway Star blocks and in the appliquéd inner border framing the appliqué. The outer border quilting has a design that echoes the triangle inside each of the triangles in the border.

3. Prepare double-fold binding with the dark green strips cut earlier. Bind the quilt top using your preferred method.

Pathways Table Runner

FINISHED SIZE: 18 ½" x 36 ½"
FINISHED BLOCK SIZE: 6" square
Designed, made and quilted by Deanne Eisenman.

When picking your fabric for this runner, choose dark and medium colors that coordinate well. The tan fabrics can be light or medium or both, your choice. The Pathway Star blocks that make up this runner will have a color print background (Block Y) and a tan print background (Block Z). There will be seven of each block type. The key to a successful scrappy look is to cut the pieces needed for each block from assorted color prints and assorted tan prints. It takes a little planning and organization, but the work will pay off.

FABRICS AND MATERIALS NEEDED

FOR PIECED TOP
- ¼ yard of a medium tan print for the center panel
- 6 Fat quarters of assorted color prints
- 6 Fat quarters of assorted tan prints
- 1 – 23" x 41" piece of batting and backing fabric
- ⅙ yard of a dark brown for single-fold binding

FOR APPLIQUÉ
- 1 – 8" x 12" piece of medium green print for stems, small calyxes and leaves
- 1 – 4½" x 6" piece of dark red for the large flowers
- 1 – 3" x 7" piece of medium gold for the large flowers and center medallion
- 1 – 3½ x 4½" piece of medium brown for the large flower calyxes
- 1 – 4" x 5" piece of medium purple for the small flowers

- 1 – 3" square piece of medium blue for the center medallion
- 1 – 1 ½" square piece dark red for the center medallion

CUTTING INSTRUCTIONS

Each block has 1 A piece, 12 B pieces, 4 C pieces, 16 D pieces and 4 E pieces. In the cutting instructions, the pieces are labeled with a letter designation that indicates which piece it is and in which block it appears. For example, piece A–Y is piece A in block Y. To maintain a scrappy look for the runner, do not cut all the same pieces from the same fabric. For example, there is a total of 112 tan print D–Y pieces for 7 Y blocks. Do not cut all 112 from the same tan print. Keep all of your pieces separated and carefully labeled for successful piecing.

FOR THE CENTER PANEL

From the medium tan print, cut:
- 1 – 6 ½" x 24 ½" rectangle

FOR THE SEVEN BLOCK Y

From the tan prints, cut a total of:
- 7 – 2 ½" squares (A–Y)
- 112 – 1 ½" squares (D–Y)

From the color prints, cut a total of:
- 28 – 1 ½" x 4 ½" rectangles (E–Y)
- 28 – 1 ½" x 2 ½" rectangles (C–Y)
- 84 – 1 ½" squares (B–Y)

FOR THE SEVEN BLOCK Z

From the tan prints, cut a total of:
- 28 – 1 ½" x 4 ½" rectangles (E–Z)
- 28 – 1 ½" x 2 ½" rectangles (C–Z)
- 84 – 1 ½" squares (B–Z)

From the color prints, cut a total of:
- 7 – 2 ½" squares (A–Z)
- 112 – 1 ½" squares (D–Z)

ADDITIONAL CUTTING

From the medium green print for stems, cut:
- 2 – ¾" x 9" bias strips
- 4 – ¾" x 5" bias strips

(See Cutting Bias Strips and Making Stems on page 23.)

Set aside the remainder of the fabric for the leaves and small calyxes to be cut later.
From the medium brown binding fabric, cut:
- 3 –1 ½" x 40" strips for single-fold binding

ASSEMBLY INSTRUCTIONS

The following instructions are for one Block Y. Repeat the following steps for a total of 7 blocks. Be sure to use an accurate ¼" seam when stitching the pieces together.

PATHWAY STARS – BLOCK Y

1. Using 4 color print B–Y pieces and a tan print A–Y piece, refer to the Square-in-a-square instructions on page 19 of General Instructions to make a Square–in–a–square unit that measures 2 ½". Do not cut off excess fabric in seam allowance until the entire unit is finished and measured.

2. Using 8 tan print D–Y pieces and 4 color print C–Y pieces, refer to the flying geese instructions on page 19 of General Instructions to make 4 flying geese units that measuren1 ½" x 2 ½".

3. Sew a color print B–Y square to each side of a flying geese unit from the previous step to make a row that measures 1 ½" x 4 ½". Make 2 rows.

4. Lay out and join the unit from step 1, the rows from step 3 and the 2 other flying geese units to construct the center of the block that will measure 4 ½" square.

5. Using 8 tan print D–Y pieces and 4 color print E–Y pieces, refer to the folded–corner technique instructions on page 19 of General Instructions to make 4 units that measure 1 ½" x 4 ½". Do not trim off the excess fabric in the seam allowance until the entire unit is finished and measured.

6. Sew a color print B–Y piece to each side of the unit from step 5 to make a row that measures 1 ½" x 6 ½". Make 2 rows.

7. Lay out and join the center of the block constructed previously, the 2 rows from step 6 and the remaining 2 units from step 5 to finish the Pathway Star - Block Y. The block should measure 6 ½" square.

PATHWAY STARS – BLOCK Z

The following instructions are for one Block Z. Repeat the following steps for a total of 7 blocks.

1. Follow step 1 of the Block Y instructions to make a Square-in-a-square center unit from a color print A–Z piece and 4 tan print B–Z pieces.

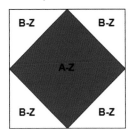

2. Follow step 2 of the Block Y instructions to make 4 flying geese units using 4 tan print C–Z and 8 color print D–Z pieces.

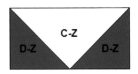

3. Follow step 3 of the Block Y instructions using 2 flying geese units from step 2 and 4 tan print B–Z pieces to make the 2 rows.

4. Follow step 4 of the Block Y instructions to make the center unit of the Block Z.

5. Follow step 5 of the Block Y instructions using 4 tan print E–Z and 8 color print D–Z pieces to make 4 units.Follow step 6 of the Block Y instructions using the units made in step 5 and 4 tan print B–Z pieces to make two rows.

6. Follow the last step of the Block Y instructions to complete Block Z.

There should now be a total of 14 blocks measuring 6 ½" square: 7 Block Y and 7 Block Z.

QUILT TOP ASSEMBLY

Before stitching the blocks into the rows, you may want to lay them out on a design wall or floor to achieve the color placement you want.

1. Join 3 Block Y and 3 Block Z into a row. Make 2 rows that measure 6 ½" x 36 ½".

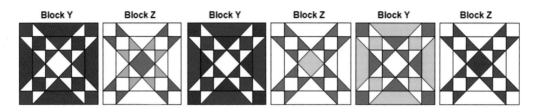

2. Join a Block Y and a Block Z to each end of the medium tan print center panel cut earlier.

3. Join the rows from steps 1 and 2 to finish the quilt top assembly.

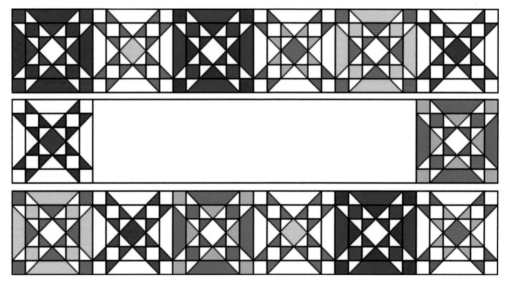

APPLIQUÉ INSTRUCTIONS

Refer to the Handy Tips on page 23 or use your preferred method of appliqué.

Appliqué templates and diagram are on page 88.

1. To make stems from the medium green print 9" and 5" bias strips, refer to Cutting Bias Strips and Making Stems on page 23.

2. Trace the appliqué shapes needed onto the designated fabric and prepare them for stitching.

3. Position and appliqué the stems in place first. The two 9" stems will radiate from the center medallion for the large flowers. The 5" stems will radiate out from the center medallion on each side of the long stems for the small flowers.

4. Position and appliqué the center medallion circles, large flowers, small flowers, calyxes and leaves

FINISHING INSTRUCTIONS

1. Layer the quilt top with batting and backing.

2. Quilt as desired. I quilted a free-hand motif in the star blocks and then loops and stars that meander around the appliqué. I echo quilted inside the appliqué, as well.

3. Prepare single-fold binding with the medium brown strips cut earlier. Bind the quilt top using your preferred method.

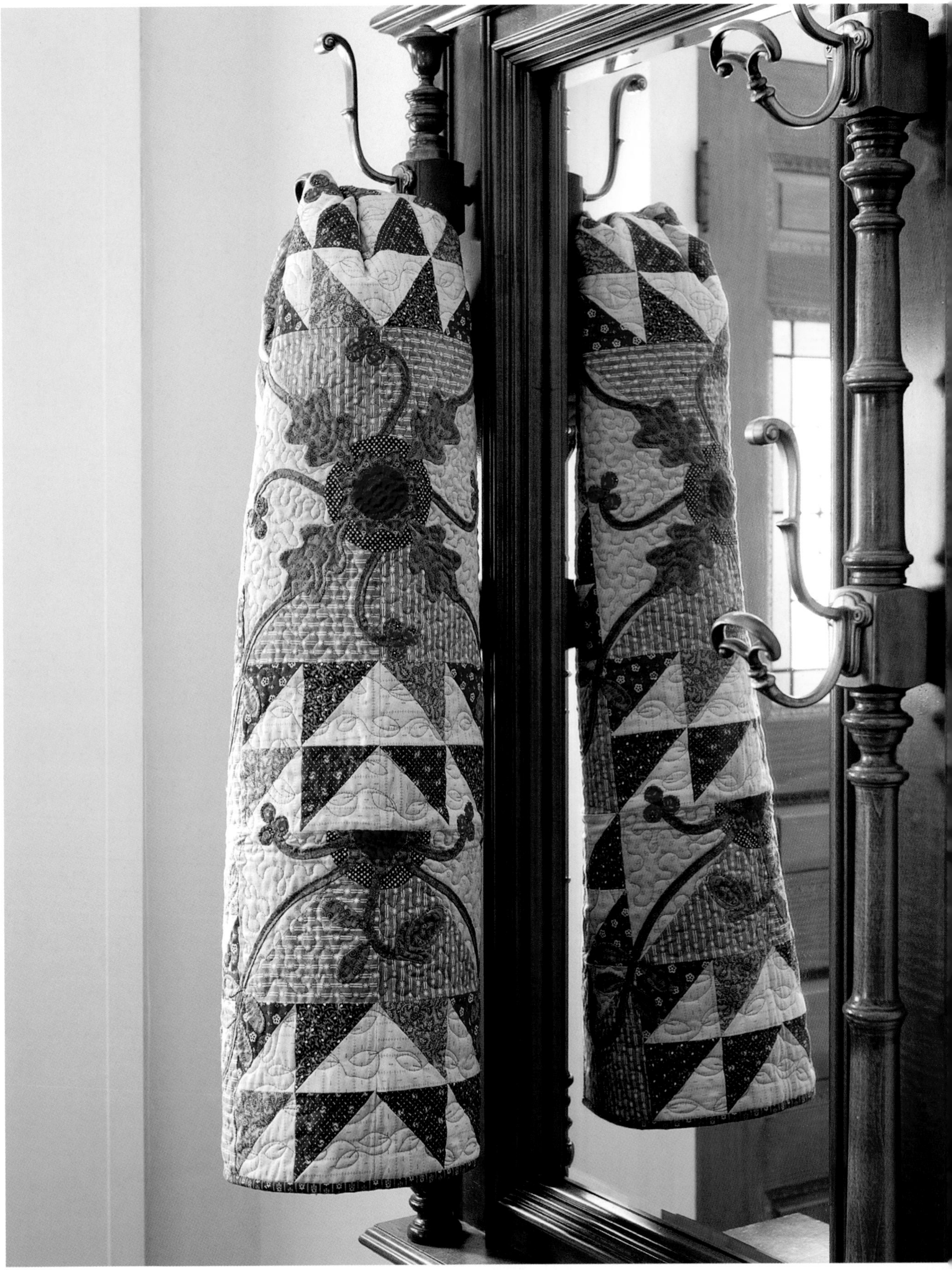

Sunburst Table Topper

FINISHED SIZE: 24 ½" x 48 ½"
FINISHED BLOCK SIZE: 12" square
Designed, made and quilted by Deanne Eisenman.

This is another quilt inspired by a block spied in an older quilt. I wanted to make a smaller version since the original quilt was queen size. Repeating the block with some clever rotation created the design I call "sunburst" since it looks like the rays of the sun when they are shooting out of a cloud. I thought these blocks were the perfect canvas for a medallion style appliqué.

FABRIC AND MATERIALS NEEDED

FOR PIECED TOP
- ½ yard medium tan print for blocks
- 4 assorted light tan print fat eighths for blocks
- ½ yard medium gold print for blocks
- 1 fat eighth each: medium red, green, purple and blue prints for blocks

FOR APPLIQUÉ
- 1 Fat eighth medium green print #1 for stems
- 1 Fat quarter medium green print #2 for large leaves, large calyxes, small leaves and small calyxes
- 1 – 8" square piece dark blue print for medallions
- 1 – 7" square piece medium brown print for medallions
- 1 – 4" square piece dark red print for medallions
- 8 assorted 3" x 4" pieces of color prints for large flowers
- 8 assorted 2" x 2 ¾" pieces color prints for large flower centers
- 2 assorted 2" x 2 ¾" pieces color prints for small flowers
- 2 assorted 1 ½" x 2" pieces color prints for small flower centers
- 1 – 7" square piece medium red print for berries

OTHER MATERIALS
- 28" x 52" piece of batting and backing fabric
- ¼ yard medium brown for single-fold binding

CUTTING INSTRUCTIONS
From the medium tan print, cut
- 8 – 6 ⅞" squares (A)

From each of the 4 light tan print fat eighths, cut:
- 8 – 3 ⅞" squares (C) for a total of 32 squares

From the medium gold print, cut:
- 8 – 6 ⅞" squares (B)

From each of the 4 color print fat eighths, cut:
- 8 – 3 ⅞" squares (D) for a total of 32 squares

From the medium green print #1, cut:
- 4 – ¾" x 13" bias strips
- 4 – ¾" x 10" bias strips
- 10 – ¾" x 6" bias strips

(See Cutting Bias Strips and Making Stems on page 23.)

From the medium brown binding fabric, cut:
- 4 – 1 ½" x 40" strips for single-fold binding

ASSEMBLY INSTRUCTIONS
SUNBURST BLOCKS

1. Using the medium tan print A squares and medium gold print B squares, refer to the Half-Square Triangle squares instructions on page 19 of General Instructions to make 16 squares.

2. Trim the squares as needed to measure 6 ½". Be sure to line up your ruler's 45-degree line with the center diagonal seam of this square to make sure it is trimmed evenly.

3. Repeat steps 1 and 2 with the light tan print C and color print D pieces for a total of 64 squares that measure 3 ½".

4. Join four different color 3 ½" squares from step 3 into a unit. Make a total of 16 units that measure 6 ½".

5. Lay out and join two 6 ½" gold/tan squares and 2 of the units from step 4 to make the Sunburst block.

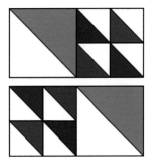

QUILT TOP ASSEMBLY

1. Join 4 Sunburst blocks into a unit that measures 24 ½". Make 2 units.

2. Sew the 2 units from step 1 together. The bottom unit will be flipped 180° so the center sunburst design is created.

APPLIQUÉ INSTRUCTIONS

Refer to the Handy Tips on page 23 or use your preferred method of appliqué.

Appliqué templates and diagrams are on page 90 and 91.

1. To make stems from the medium green #1 print 13", 10" and 6" bias strips, refer to Cutting Bias Strips and Making Stems on page 23.

2. Trace the appliqué shapes onto the designated fabric and prepare them for stitching.

FOR THE APPLIQUÉ CENTER

1. Position and appliqué the center stems (refer to diagram) first. Then stitch the blue medallion center to cover the raw ends of the stems.

2. Next, position and stitch the large leaves, then the remainder of the center medallion to cover the raw ends of the leaves.

3. Stitch the large calyxes to the ends of the long stems and then stitch the large flowers in place.

4. Stitch the berries to the ends of the small stems.

5. Last, stitch the small leaves in place.

FOR THE APPLIQUÉ ENDS

1. Stitch the blue print half circles where shown on the diagram.

2. Position and stitch the stems, then stitch down the remainder of the medallion to cover the raw ends of the stems.

3. Stitch the large and small calyxes to the ends of the stems and then the flowers.

4. Last, stitch the berries and small leaves.

FINISHING INSTRUCTIONS

1. Layer the quilt top with batting and backing.

2. Quilt as desired. I did a free-motion leaf design and a free-motion meandering stitch in the open spaces. I echo quilted inside the appliqués for definition.

3. Prepare single-fold binding with the medium brown strips cut earlier. Bind the quilt top using your preferred method.

Wind Farm

FINISHED SIZE: 62" square Lap Quilt
FINISHED BLOCK SIZE: 12" square
Designed and made by Deanne Eisenman and quilted by Annette Ashbach of The Quiltmaker's Nest.

Wind Farm is another quilt that was inspired by a block found in an antique quilt. The original block was on point with the flying geese rows forming an "X" in the block. I decided to turn the block and add the corners to give it the illusion of being on point. This is my version of an early 19th century block style quilt with added appliqué in the borders.

FABRICS AND MATERIALS NEEDED
FOR PIECED TOP
- ⅝ yard dark red print #1 for Block Y
- ⅝ yard dark red print #2 for Block Z
- ⅜ yard medium blue print #1 for Block Y and pieced inner border
- ⅜ yard medium gold print for Block Y and pieced inner border
- ⅜ yard medium purple print for Block Z and pieced inner border
- ⅜ yard medium green print for Block Z and pieced inner border
- ½ yard light tan print #1 for Block Y
- ¾ yard light tan print # 2 for Block Y
- ½ yard light tan print #3 for Block Z
- ¾ yard light tan print #4 for Block Z
- 1 yard medium tan print for pieced inner border
- ⅔ yard medium blue print #2 for outer border

OTHER MATERIALS
- 74" square piece of batting and backing
- ½ yard dark blue print for double-fold binding

FOR APPLIQUÉ
- 1 Fat quarter medium green print for stems and leaves
- 1 – 8" x 12" piece medium blue print for large flowers
- 1 – 11" x 12" piece medium pink print for large and small flowers
- 1 – 3" x 8" piece light gold print for large flowers
- 1 – 5" x 10" piece dark brown print #1 for large and small flowers
- 1 – 4" square of dark brown print #2 for penny circles
- 1 – 2½" square of dark red print for penny circles

CUTTING INSTRUCTIONS

From the dark red print #1, cut:
- 96 – 2" x 3 ½" rectangles (B–Y)

From the dark red print #2, cut:
- 96 – 2" x 3 ½" rectangles (B–Z)

From the medium blue print #1, cut:
- 11 – 5 ¾" squares; cut diagonally twice for 44 quarter-square triangles (E–Y)

From the medium gold print, cut:
- 11– 5 ¾" squares; cut diagonally twice for 44 quarter-square triangles (F–Y)

From the medium purple print, cut:
- 11 – 5 ¾" squares; cut diagonally twice for 44 quarter-square triangles (E–Z)

From the medium green print, cut:
- 11 – 5 ¾" squares; cut diagonally twice for 44 quarter-square triangles (F–Z)

From the light tan print #1, cut:
- 16 – 5 ⅜" squares; cut diagonally once for 32 half-square triangles (D–Y)

From the light tan print #2, cut:
- 8 – 3 ½" squares (A-Y)
- 192 – 2" squares (C-Y)

From the light tan print #3, cut:
- 16 – 5 ⅜" squares; cut diagonally once for 32 half-square triangles (D-Z)

From the light tan print #4, cut:
- 8 – 3 ½" squares (A-Z)
- 192 – 2" squares (C-Z)

From the medium tan print, cut:
- 12 – 5 ⅜" squares; cut diagonally once for 24 half-square triangles (G)
- 4 – 5" x 12 ½" rectangles (J)
- 4 – 5" x 8" rectangles (I)
- 8 – 3" ½ x 5" rectangles (H)

From the medium blue print #2, cut:
- 4 – 2 ¾" x 31 ¼" strips
- 4 – 2 ¾" x 29" strips

From the dark blue binding fabric, cut:
- 7 – 2 ½" x 40" strips for double-fold binding

From the medium green print fat quarter, cut:
- 8 – 1" x 10 ½" bias strips
- 8 – 1" x 7 ½" bias strips

(See Cutting Bias Strips and Making Stems on page 23.)

Set aside the remainder of the fabric for additional appliqué pieces to be cut later.

ASSEMBLY INSTRUCTIONS

WIND FARM BLOCKS

There are two color schemes for these blocks. Eight will have blue and gold corner squares (Block Y) and 8 will have purple and green corner squares (Block Z). The following instructions are for Block Y. Repeat the instructions to make Block Z using the pieces cut for that block.

1. Using the light tan print #2 C-Y squares and the red print #1 B-Y rectangles, refer to the Flying Geese Instructions on page 19 of General Instructions to make 96 flying geese units that measure 2" x 3 ½".

2. Join 3 flying geese units into a row that measures 3 ½" x 5". Make a total of 32 rows. Set these units aside for the block assembly that starts in step 6.

3. Join a medium blue print #1 E-Y piece and a medium gold F-Y piece. Make a total of 44 units. Set 12 of these units aside for the pieced border assembly and label them Unit K.

4. Join a light tan print #1 D-Y piece to a blue/gold unit from step 3 to make a square that measures 5". Make a total of 32 squares.

5. Sew a blue/gold square from step 4 to each side of a flying geese row from step 2 to make a row that measures 5" x 12 ½". Make 2 rows.

6. Sew 2 flying geese rows from step 2 to each side of a light tan print #2 A-Y piece to make a row that measures 3 ½" x 12 ½". Make 1 row.

7. Join the rows from steps 5 and 6 to make a Block Y that measures 12 ½" square.

8. Repeat steps 5 through 7 to make a total of 8 Block Y.
9. Follow steps 1 through 7 with the Block Z pieces in place of the Block Y pieces to make 8 Block Z.

QUILT TOP CENTER ASSEMBLY

1. Join 2 Block Y and 2 Block Z into a row that measures 12 ½" x 48 ½". Make 4 rows.
2. Join the 4 rows from steps 1 to make the quilt top center. The second and the fourth row are flipped 180 degrees so that they begin with a Block Z.

PIECED INNER BORDER

1. Join a medium tan print G piece to a blue/gold K unit, set aside earlier, to make a square measuring 5". Make a total of 12 squares. Repeat this step with the purple/green K units and the remaining medium tan print G pieces. Make a total of 12 squares.

2. Join a purple/green square and a blue/gold square from step 1. Make 6 units measuring 5" x 9 ½" and label them K1.

3. Repeat step 2 with the remaining purple/green and blue/gold squares except the blue/gold square will be on the left side. Make 6 units measuring 5" x 9 ½" and label them K2.

4. Join 2 K1 units and 1 K2 unit with 2 medium tan H and 2 medium tan I pieces to make a row. Make 2 rows.

5. Join 1 K1 unit and 2 K2 units with 2 medium tan H and 2 medium tan J pieces to make a row. Make 2 rows.

6. Sew the rows from step 4 to the top and bottom of the quilt top center. Sew the rows from step 5 to the sides of the quilt top center.

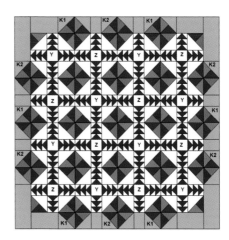

OUTER BORDER

1. Join 2 medium blue print 2 ¾" x 29" strips at the ends to make one 57 ½" border strip. Make 2.
2. Repeat step 1 with 2 medium blue print 2 ¾" x 31 ¼" strips to make one 62" border strip. Make 2.
3. Sew the border strips from step 1 to the sides of the quilt top center and then sew the border strips from step 2 to the top and bottom of the quilt top center.

FINISHING INSTRUCTIONS

1. Layer the quilt top with batting and backing.
2. Quilt as desired. Annette quilted a large free-motion flower motif in the Wind Farm blocks and a meandering loop pattern in the borders.
3. Prepare double-fold binding with the dark blue strips cut earlier. Bind the quilt top using your preferred method.

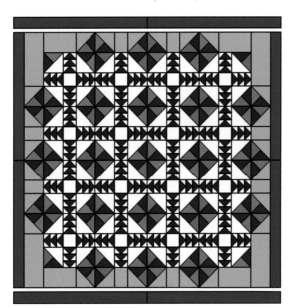

APPLIQUÉ INSTRUCTIONS

Refer to the Handy Tips on page 23 or use your preferred method of appliqué. Appliqué templates and diagrams are on page 93 and 94.

1. To make stems from the 1" x 10 ½" and 1" x 7 ½" bias strips, refer to Cutting Bias Strips and Making Stems on page 23.
2. Trace the appliqué shapes needed onto the designated fabrics and prepare them for stitching.
3. Position and appliqué the stems in place first referring to the diagram. Since the corner appliqués and the center border appliqués are all the same, the appliqué diagram will show these sections just once. After appliquéing the stems, stitch the flowers, leaves and penny circles. Finally, embroider the flower stamens using black embroidery floss and a simple back stitch. Top off the stamens with French knots.

Nine Patch Garden

FINISHED SIZE: 68" square Lap Quilt
FINISHED BLOCK SIZE: 12" square
Designed and made by Deanne Eisenman

Quilted by Annette Ashbach of The Quiltmaker's Nest

This quilt was also inspired by the early block style quilts. Instead of adding appliqué to plain borders around the quilt, I wanted to weave appliqué through the quilt, almost like floral vines winding beside a garden path.

FABRICS AND MATERIALS NEEDED

FOR PIECED TOP

- ⅓ yard each of 9 assorted dark or medium color prints for Nine-Patch Star blocks

- 1 yard each of 3 assorted tan prints for Nine-Patch Star blocks

- ⅝ yard black print for Nine-Patch setting blocks

- ⅝ yard light or medium tan print #1 for Nine-Patch setting blocks

- ⅝ yard light or medium tan print #2 for Nine-Patch setting blocks

- 1 ½ yards medium brown print for setting triangles

FOR APPLIQUÉ

- ½ yard medium green print for stems, leaves and calyxes

- 1 Fat eighth medium red print for berries

- 3 – 6" x 8" pieces of assorted light color prints for large flowers and large flower centers

- 3 – 6" x 8" pieces of assorted medium color prints for large flowers and large flower centers

- 1 – 6" x 8 ½" piece of medium blue for small flowers

- 1 – 3" x 4 ½" piece of medium gold for small flowers

OTHER MATERIALS

- 80" square piece of batting and backing fabric

- ½ yard black print for double-fold binding

CUTTING INSTRUCTIONS

NINE-PATCH STAR BLOCKS

For the Nine-Patch Star blocks, sort your ⅓ yard color prints into 3 sets of 3 coordinating fabrics and pair each stack with a 1 yard tan print.

Label the sets Set #1, Set #2 and Set # 3. There are a total of 16 of these blocks. One set of fabric will produce 6 blocks while the other 2 sets will produce 5 blocks each.

Cut the A and D pieces for the block from assorted color prints within the set so your blocks are scrappy. It takes a little math and planning, but once that part is done, the rest is a breeze.

SET #1

From the assorted color prints, cut a total of:
- 12 – 5 ¼" squares; cut diagonally twice for 48 quarter-square triangles (D)
- 30 – 4 ½" squares (A)

From the tan print, cut:
- 12 – 5 ¼" squares; cut diagonally twice for 48 quarter square triangles (C)
- 120 – 2 ½" squares (B)

SET #2

From the assorted color prints, cut a total of:
- 10 – 5 ¼" squares; cut diagonally twice for 40 quarter square triangles (D)
- 25 – 4 ½" squares (A)

From the tan print, cut:
- 10 – 5 ¼" squares; cut diagonally twice for 40 quarter square triangles (C)
- 100 – 2 ½" squares (B)

- **SET #3**

From the assorted color prints, cut a total of:
- 10 – 5 ¼" squares; cut diagonally twice for 40 quarter square triangles (D)
- 25 – 4 ½" squares (A)

From the tan print, cut:
- 10 – 5 ¼" squares; cut diagonally twice for 40 quarter square triangles (C)
- 100 – 2 ½" squares (B)

NINE-PATCH SETTING BLOCKS

From the light/medium tan print #1, cut:
- 7 – 2 ½" x 40" strips (F)

From the black print, cut:
- 8 – 2 ½" x 40" strips (E)

From the light/medium tan print #2, cut:
- 18 – 6 ½" squares (G)

SETTING TRIANGLES

- 2 – 18 ¼" squares; cut diagonally twice for 8 quarter-square triangles (I) (you will use 6)
- 3 – 9 ¾" squares; cut diagonally twice for 12 quarter-square triangles (H)
- 2 – 9 ⅜" squares; cut diagonally once for 4 half-square triangles (J)

ADDITIONAL CUTTING

- Cut the ½ yard medium green print (for appliqué) into 2 fat quarters (18" x 20"). Set aside 1 of the fat quarters for the appliqué section of this pattern.

From the remaining medium green fat quarter, cut:
- 12 – ¾" x 18" bias strips
- 4 – ¾" x 10" bias strips
- 2 – ¾" x 7" bias strips
- 4 – ¾" x 4" bias strips
(See Cutting Bias Strips and Making Stems on page 23.)

From the black print binding fabric, cut
- 7 – 2 ½" x 40" stripes for double-fold binding

ASSEMBLY INSTRUCTIONS

NINE-PATCH STAR BLOCKS

The following instructions are for 1 block. Repeat these instructions to make all 16 blocks that measure 12 ½" square.

1. Using a color print A square and 4 tan print B squares, refer to the Square-in-a-square instructions on page 19 to make a unit that measures 4 ½" square. Do not trim off the excess fabric until the whole unit is complete and measured. Repeat this step for a total of 5 Square-in-a-square units using the same color print A square.

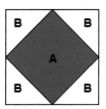

2. Join a tan print C piece and a color print D piece (different color from the A piece used in step 1) to make a unit. Make a total of 8 units.

3. Join 2 of the units from step 4 into a square. Make 4 units that measure 4 ½" square.

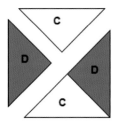

4. Lay out and join the units from step 1 and the units from step 3 to construct the Nine-Patch Star block.

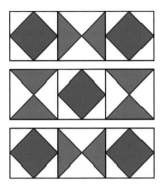

5. Repeat steps 1 through 4 to make a total of 16 blocks.

NINE-PATCH SETTING BLOCKS

1. Using 2 black print 40" strips and a tan print #1 40" strip, refer to the Strip Set Instructions on page 18 to make a strip set with the tan print #1 strip between the black print strips. Make a total of 3 of these strips sets.

2. Cut the strip sets from step 1 into 2 ½" x 6 ½" segments. Cut a total of 48 segments.

3. Repeat step 1 with 2 tan print #1 40" strips and a black print 40" strip to make a strip set with the black print strip between the tan print #1 strips. Make a total of 2 of these strip sets.

4. Cut the strips sets from step 3 into 2 ½" x 6 ½" segments. Cut a total of 24 segments.

5. Join 2 units from step 2 and 1 unit from step 4 to make a Nine-Patch unit. Make a total of 24 units that measure 6 ½" square. Set aside 6 of these units for the Nine-Patch Setting Triangles.

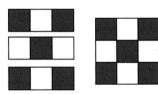

6. Lay out and join 2 Nine-Patch units and 2 tan print #2 G squares to construct a Nine-Patch setting block that measures 12 ½" square. Make a total of 9 setting blocks.

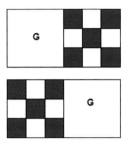

NINE-PATCH SETTING TRIANGLES

1. Lay a medium brown H triangle face down on a Nine-Patch unit that was set aside in the previous section. Line up the 90 degree angle of the triangle with the corner of the Nine-Patch unit. The other points of the triangle will overlap the block a bit.

2. Sew the triangle and block together and press open. Do not clip off the overlapping points at this time.

3. Repeat steps 1 and 2 on the adjacent side of the Nine-Patch unit. Sew the triangle and block together and press open. At this time, you can clip off the overlapping points if desired.

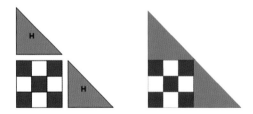

Repeat steps 1 through 3 to make a total of 6 of these Nine-Patch setting triangles.

QUILT TOP ASSEMBLY

Before assembling the rows to construct the quilt top, plan color placement by looking at the piecing diagram to determine where you want to place each of your blocks. Using a design wall or a large floor space is helpful. The rows will be pieced diagonally using the blocks and setting triangles to achieve the on-point setting of this quilt.

1. Join a Nine-Patch Star block, a Nine-Patch setting triangle, a medium brown J and a medium brown I piece to make a row. Make 2 rows and label them Row A.

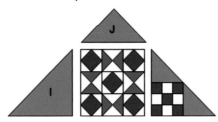

2. Join 2 Nine-Patch Star blocks, a Nine-Patch setting block, a Nine-Patch setting triangle and a medium brown I piece to make a row. Make 2 rows and label them Row B.

3. Join 3 Nine-Patch Star blocks, 2 Nine-Patch setting blocks, a Nine-Patch setting triangle and a medium brown I piece to make a row. Make 2 rows and label them Row C.

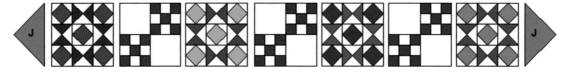

4. Join 4 Nine-Patch Star blocks, 3 Nine-Patch setting blocks and 2 medium brown J pieces to make a row. Make 1 row and label it Row D.

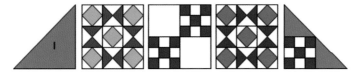

5. Lay out the rows from steps 1 through 4. Note that the A, B and C rows on the bottom are flipped 180 degrees from the A, B and C rows on the top.

6. Join the rows to complete the quilt top.

APPLIQUÉ INSTRUCTIONS

Appliqué templates and diagram are on page 95 and 96.

1. Make stems from the ¾" bias strips following the instructions on page 23.

2. Trace the appliqué shapes needed onto the designated fabrics and prepare them for stitching.

3. Position and appliqué the stems in place first, referring to the diagram. After appliquéing the stems, stitch the large and small flowers, calyxes, leaves and berries.

FINISHING INSTRUCTIONS

1. Layer the quilt top with batting and backing.

2. Quilt as desired. Annette quilted a free-motion star motif and feather motif in the Nine-Patch Star blocks and a free-motion petal motif in the Nine-Patch setting blocks. She also quilted a meandering loop pattern in the borders and outlined the appliqué.

3. Prepare double-fold binding with the dark blue strips cut earlier. Bind the quilt top using your preferred method.

Star Gazing Templates

Large Flower: Cut 4
from gold print #1

Large Flower: Cut 4 from
medium blue print

Large Flower Calyx:
Cut 4 from dark green
print #3

Small Flower: Cut 8
from dark brown print

Large Flower: Cut 4
from black print

Star: Cut 8 from
gold print #2

Small Flower: Cut 8
from assorted color prints

Berries: Cut 24 from
dark red print

Leaf: Cut 40 from
dark print #2

Star Gazing
Placement Diagram

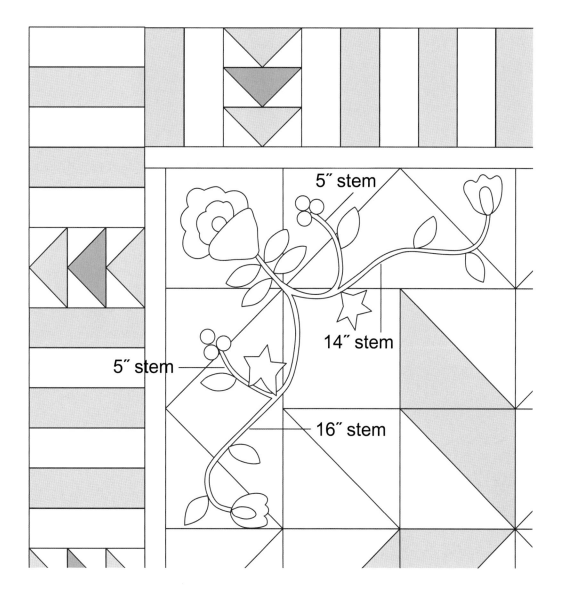

5″ stem

14″ stem

5″ stem

16″ stem

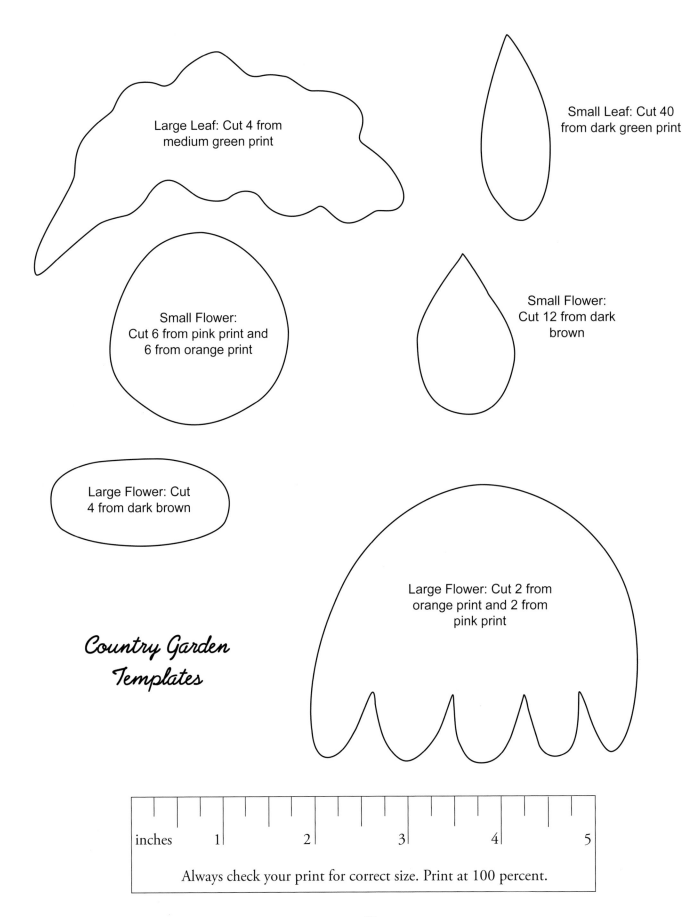

Large Leaf: Cut 4 from medium green print

Small Leaf: Cut 40 from dark green print

Small Flower: Cut 6 from pink print and 6 from orange print

Small Flower: Cut 12 from dark brown

Large Flower: Cut 4 from dark brown

Large Flower: Cut 2 from orange print and 2 from pink print

Country Garden Templates

inches   1   2   3   4   5

Always check your print for correct size. Print at 100 percent.

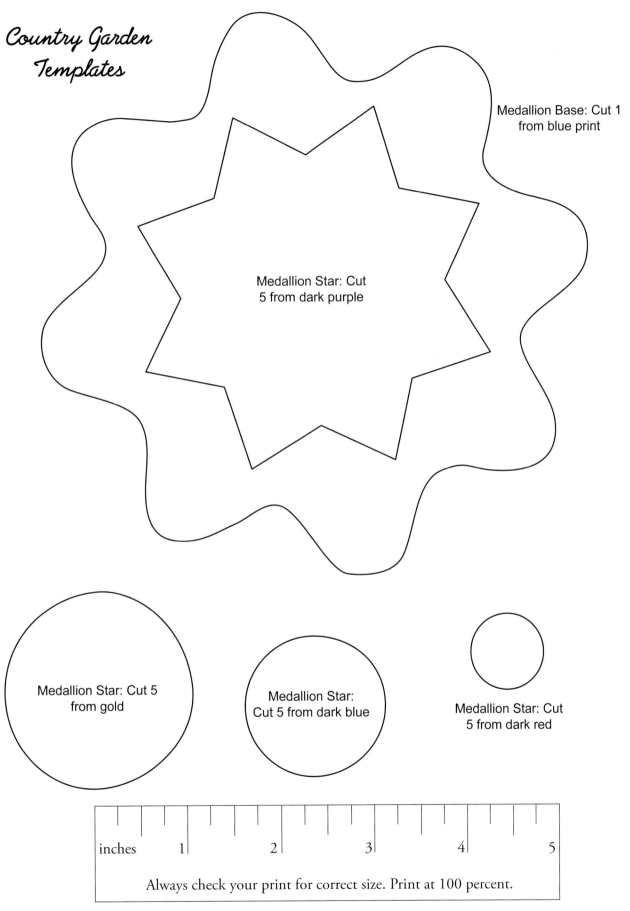

Country Garden
Templates

Medallion Base: Cut 1
from blue print

Medallion Star: Cut
5 from dark purple

Medallion Star: Cut 5
from gold

Medallion Star:
Cut 5 from dark blue

Medallion Star: Cut
5 from dark red

inches   1   2   3   4   5

Always check your print for correct size. Print at 100 percent.

Country Garden
Appliqué Diagram

Summer Evening Blooms
Templates

Large Flower: Cut 4 from dark brown #1 print

Large Flower: Cut 4 from various color prints

Large Flower: Cut 4 from various color prints

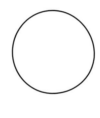

Large Flower: Cut 4 from various color prints
Small Flower: Cut 12 from dark brown #2 print
Berries: Cut 12 from dark red

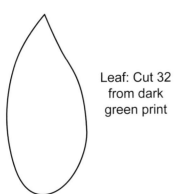

Leaf: Cut 32 from dark green print

Small Flower: Cut 12 from various color prints

Summer Evening Blooms
Appliqué Placement Diagram

Open Windows Templates

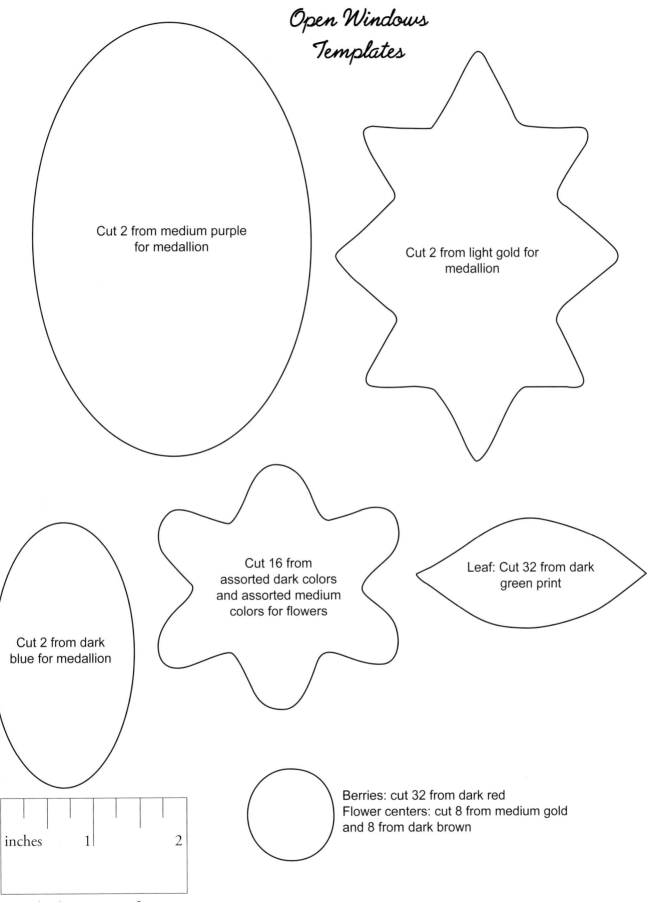

Cut 2 from medium purple for medallion

Cut 2 from light gold for medallion

Cut 16 from assorted dark colors and assorted medium colors for flowers

Leaf: Cut 32 from dark green print

Cut 2 from dark blue for medallion

Berries: cut 32 from dark red
Flower centers: cut 8 from medium gold and 8 from dark brown

inches   1   2

Always check your print for correct size.
Print at 100 percent.

Open Windows
Appliqué Placement Diagram

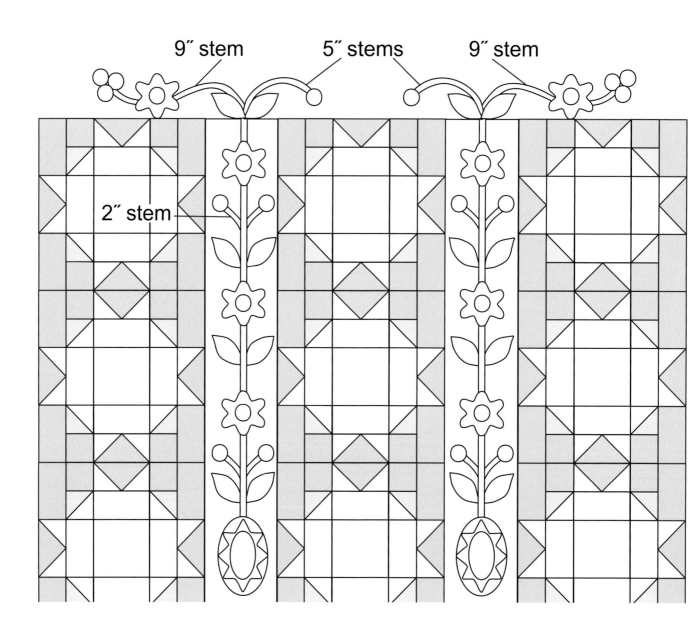

9″ stem   5″ stems   9″ stem

2″ stem

Pathways Lap Quilt
Templates

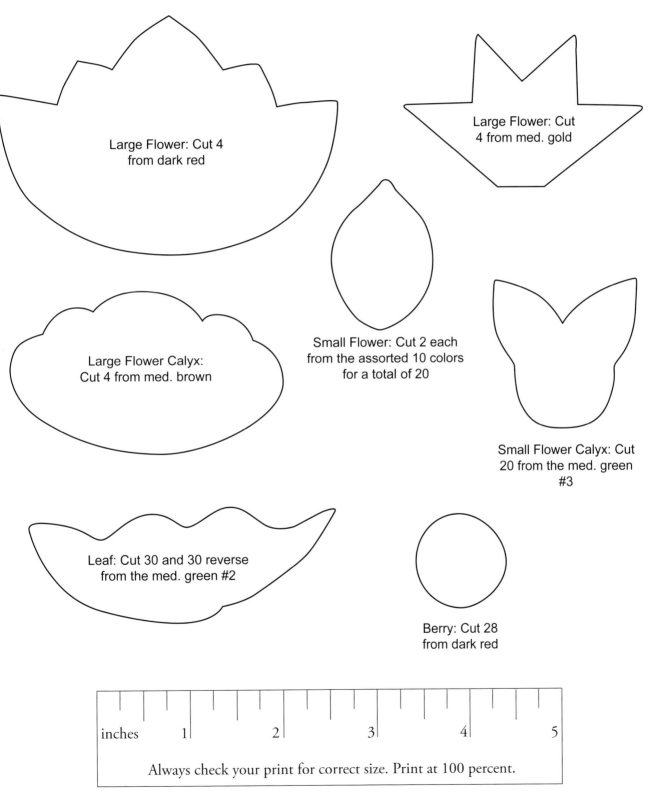

Large Flower: Cut 4
from dark red

Large Flower: Cut
4 from med. gold

Large Flower Calyx:
Cut 4 from med. brown

Small Flower: Cut 2 each
from the assorted 10 colors
for a total of 20

Small Flower Calyx: Cut
20 from the med. green
#3

Leaf: Cut 30 and 30 reverse
from the med. green #2

Berry: Cut 28
from dark red

inches   1   2   3   4   5

Always check your print for correct size. Print at 100 percent.

*Pathways Lap Quilt
Appliqué Placement Diagram*

*Pathways Table Runner
Appliqué Placement Diagram*

Pathways Table Runner Templates

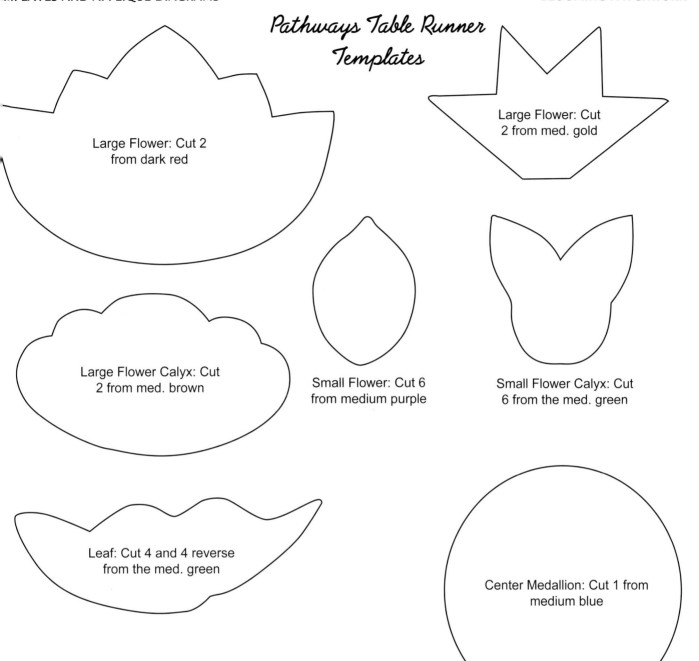

Large Flower: Cut 2
from dark red

Large Flower: Cut
2 from med. gold

Large Flower Calyx: Cut
2 from med. brown

Small Flower: Cut 6
from medium purple

Small Flower Calyx: Cut
6 from the med. green

Leaf: Cut 4 and 4 reverse
from the med. green

Center Medallion: Cut 1 from
medium blue

Center Medallion:
Cut 1 from medium
gold

Center
Medallion: Cut
1 from dark red

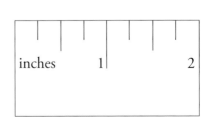

inches   1   2

Always check your print for correct size.
Print at 100 percent.

Sunburst
Templates

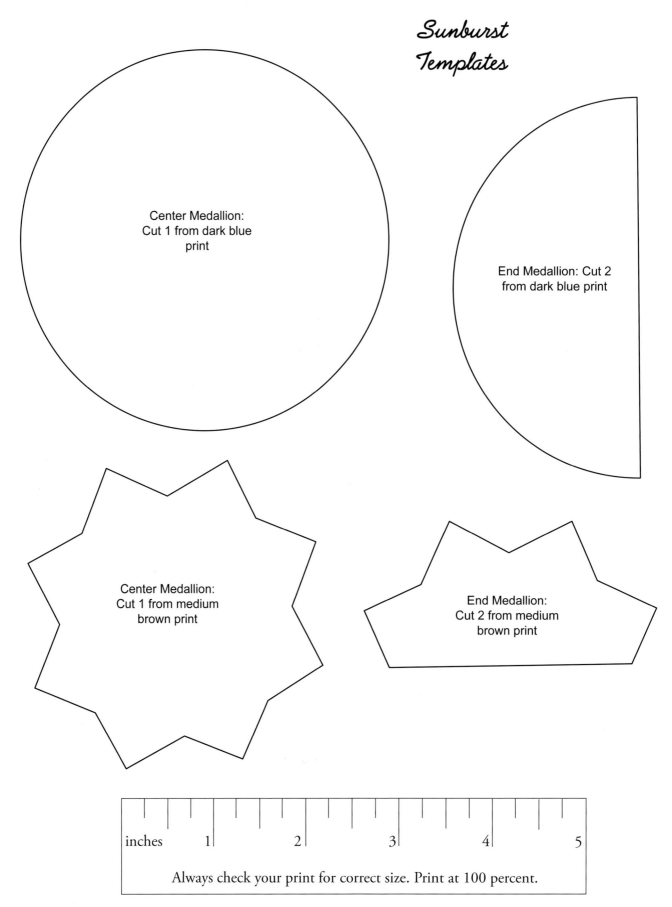

Center Medallion:
Cut 1 from dark blue
print

End Medallion: Cut 2
from dark blue print

Center Medallion:
Cut 1 from medium
brown print

End Medallion:
Cut 2 from medium
brown print

inches 1 2 3 4 5

Always check your print for correct size. Print at 100 percent.

Sunburst Templates

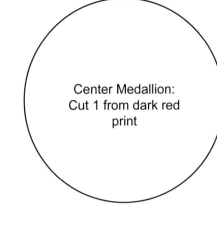

Center Medallion:
Cut 1 from dark red
print

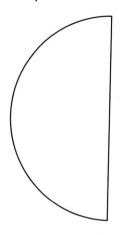

End Medallion: Cut 2
from dark red print

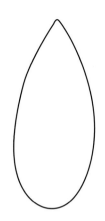

Small Leaf: Cut 28
from medium green
#2 print

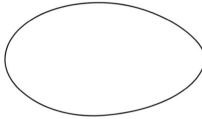

Large Flower Center: Cut 8 from
assorted color prints
Small Flowers: Cut 2 from assorted
color prints

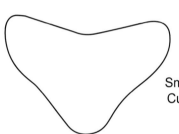

Small Flower Calyx:
Cut 2 from medium
green #2 print

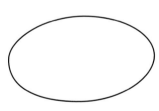

Small Flower Center:
Cut 2 from assorted
color prints

Large Flower: Cut 8 from
assorted color prints

inches   1   2   3   4   5

Always check your print for correct size. Print at 100 percent.

Sunburst Templates

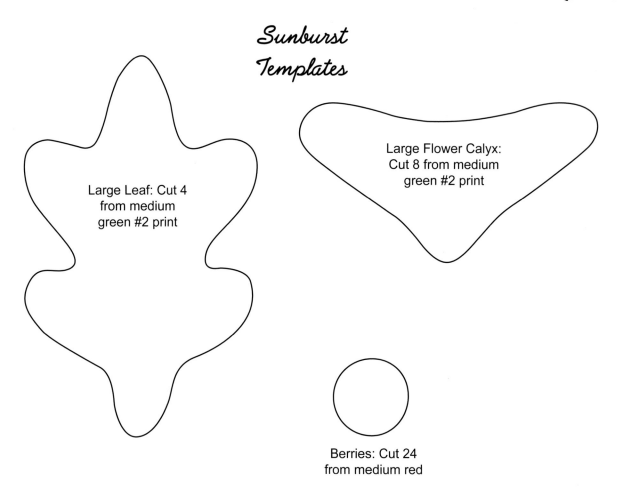

Large Leaf: Cut 4 from medium green #2 print

Large Flower Calyx: Cut 8 from medium green #2 print

Berries: Cut 24 from medium red

Sunburst Appliqué Placement Diagram

13″ bias stems   10″ bias stems   6″ bias stems

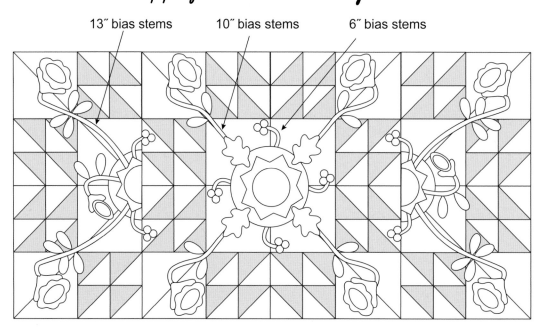

Wind Farm Templates

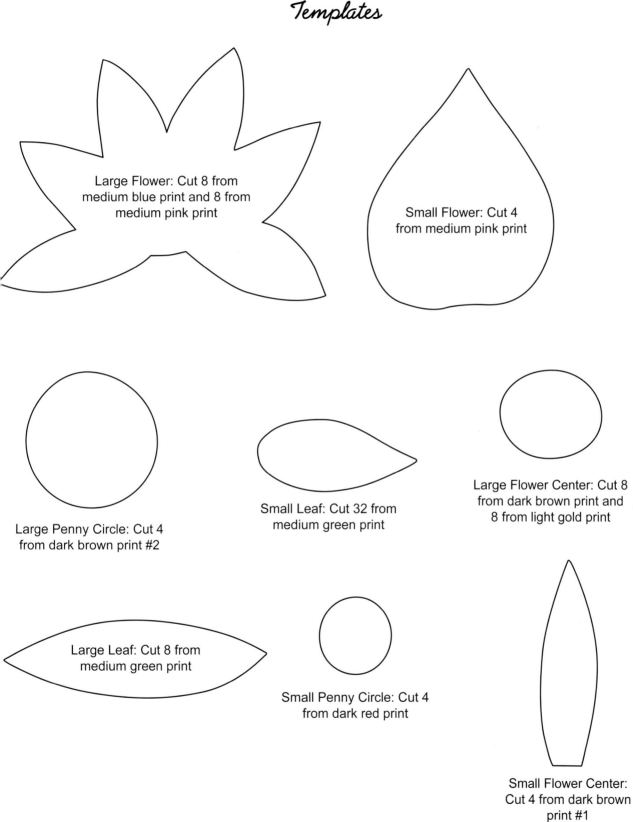

Large Flower: Cut 8 from medium blue print and 8 from medium pink print

Small Flower: Cut 4 from medium pink print

Large Penny Circle: Cut 4 from dark brown print #2

Small Leaf: Cut 32 from medium green print

Large Flower Center: Cut 8 from dark brown print and 8 from light gold print

Large Leaf: Cut 8 from medium green print

Small Penny Circle: Cut 4 from dark red print

Small Flower Center: Cut 4 from dark brown print #1

Wind Farm
Appliqué Placement Diagrams

Embroidery　　　10½″ stems

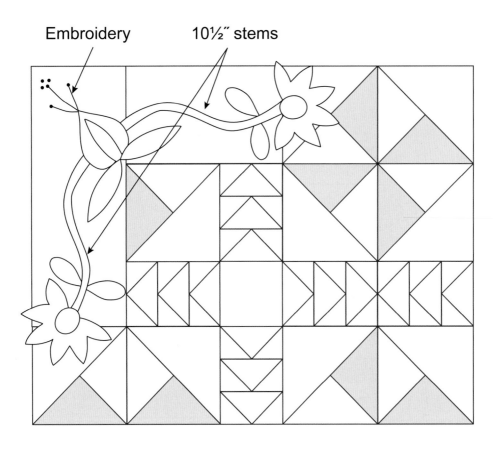

7½″ stems

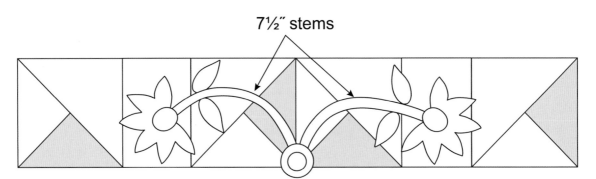

Center Inner Border Appliqué

Nine-Patch Garden Templates

Large Flower: Cut 2 from each color print for a total of 12 flowers

Large Flower Center: Cut 2 from each color print for a total of 12

Large Flower Calyx: Cut 12 from medium green print

Small Flower: Cut 6 from medium blue print

Small Flower Center: Cut 6 from medium gold print
Berries: Cut 48 from medium red print

Leaf: Cut 40 from medium green print

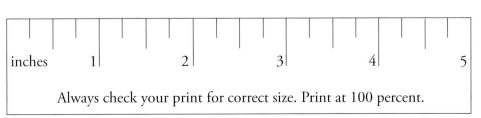

inches   1   2   3   4   5

Always check your print for correct size. Print at 100 percent.

Nine-Patch Garden
Appliqué Placement Diagram

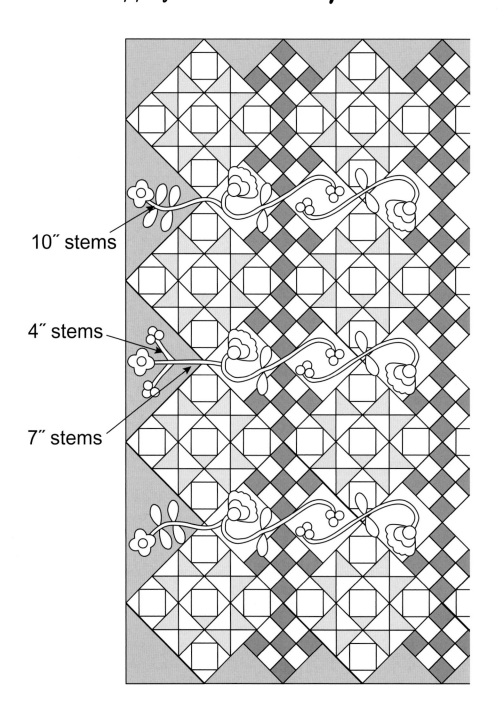

10˝ stems

4˝ stems

7˝ stems